HOMEBOYS
IN COLLEGE

Also by Hilary Paul McGuire

Hopie and the Los Homes Gang: A Gangland Primer, 1979

Hopie and the Los Homes Gang: A Gangland Primer,
Second Edition, 2012

Tennis Saves: Stewart Orphans Take World by Racket, 2012

HOMEBOYS

IN COLLEGE

HERALDS OF PROGRESS

Commemorative Thirtieth Anniversary Edition

Hilary Paul McGuire

CONTENTS

LIST OF PHOTOGRAPHS

all of which are by author except as noted.

INTRODUCTION

This book is a witness to a remarkable sociological phenomenon. For more than fifty years the Mexican-American population has had a rowdy, sometimes lawless, sub-element amounting to a mere one or two percent of the total Chicano population. Small though this element is, due to the fascination human beings have with the outlaw and the sensationalist, historians, journalists, and sociologists have often focused on it until the general Chicano population has begun to cry, "Enough, we are not represented by these renegades."

Be that as it may, this tiny subculture has been so noticeable by reason of its creative, artistic, and macho styles, (not to mention its famed juvenile delinquency), that it has always captured the imagination of other human beings and is likely to continue to do so for years to come.

Through the years this sub-element has evolved, perhaps more than most elements of society, and, as it has done so, it has given itself a variety of names: *pachuco*, zoot-suiter, *cholo*, and homeboy.

The sociological change to which this volume attests is that, in the 1980s, this sub-element in its current form, the homeboy, is responding to its own creative urges and is seeking American higher education. During all of its previous history, this subculture has been noted for its extreme alienation, not only from the general American society, but also from its own Mexican-American population.

Now, however, the homeboy has declared himself to be part of the decade of the Chicano and is throwing all of his intellectual and spiritual *fuerza* (force) as well as his dynamic physical capabilities into the fight for the advancement of his people and his neighborhood.

There is a tremendous ground-swell among the whole Chicano community in the 1980s. They themselves have decreed the '80s to be their decade. With this surge there is a growing social and political awareness. That demands education.

The homeboy, however, a minority among a minority, though he feels the tug of the tide, does not surrender himself to it in the same way. From what my homeboy friends tell me, and what I know of their fierce determination and their loyalty to their barrios, they will not be the kind of Chicano who obtains education and a fine job, then turns his back on his barrio. Once he has imbibed the affluence of American society, his loyalty will require him to reach back into his barrio and help give it and his people a grand regeneration.

He will not even forget his ancestors and relatives in Mexico. Other nationalities coming to this country have left their roots far behind, but the proximity of Mexico makes this a different situation. Besides that, the deep familial spirit of the homeboy will prompt him to spread his prosperity all the way back to Mexico.

Perhaps Mexico's greatest hope for the improvement of the financial crisis it faces in the early 1980s is to be found in the personal growth of her *carnales* (friends of the same flesh) in America.

I predict that the number of homeboys going to college will expand rapidly in the '80s and thereafter. My experience in Los Angeles in the early '70s and in San Diego in the late '70s attests that a *cholo* in those days (except for about one in a hundred), would never have considered going to college. But the '80s are an entirely different story.

That story is found in this book, but before we start it, a bit more explanation may be helpful.

The term homeboy, homie, or simply homes is one widely used by street people in Southern California. Like much street language, its origins are shrouded in obscurity. Though it is currently in use by several ethnic groups on the streets, we will use it here to refer to members of Mexican-American street gangs.

For these youths, their neighborhood (barrio) is more psychically important than a mere hangout, turf, or territory. Their neighborhood is an extension of their very home life. The barrio is a surrogate home. Hence the appropriateness of calling a fellow gang member "homeboy" or of hailing him on the street with an expression like, "Hey, homes, what's happening, man?"

During the past twelve years, I have been associated with, lived in, and taught in barrios in East Los Angeles and San Diego. In all of these years, since 1971, the word homeboy has been used in the barrio. Some youths feel so out of touch with their own parents, who speak only Spanish in some instances and cling to Mexican culture and mores, that their greatest allegiance is to their fellow *vatos* (dudes) on the street. Some feel more at home with their homies on the street corner than they do hanging around the house.

According to Mr. Raul Portillo of the San Diego Street Youth Program, he was using the word homeboy as far back as the 1940s when he was in reform school in Texas. He says, "There were *vatos* from all over the place so when we found someone from our own hometown, we called him our homeboy." It is not difficult to see how a youth, once released from such incarceration, would come back to his own neighborhood and hail all of his friends, mostly from the same gang, as homeboys.

Of course the younger boys, though they may have never been in prison, would adopt the word to express their good feelings when encountering a friend from their own neighborhood.

From the outset I want to assure my readers that there are many interpretations of the word "gang". Everyone who uses that word gives it a personal connotation. I prefer not to use the word at all due to its negative implications. I use it briefly here only to make my subject unmistakable.

In Los Angeles where I lived the experiences which I have recorded in my earlier book, *Hopie and the Los Homes Gang*, the word gang usually refers to a far more violent segment of society than it does in San Diego. San Diego lacks the hectic pressures which characterize life in the LA barrios. Less freeways, less traffic on the ones there are, less people everywhere means less pollution in San Diego and hence a much more comfortable existence which makes people feel more "laid back," less inclined to anger and violence. When life is comfortable, people are not faced to such a great extent with the hopelessness which spawns anger and crime.

East Los Angeles, which is often thought of as the capitol of Mexican-American gang activity, is about eighteen miles from the nearest beach. That is a long distance from a fresh sea breeze when one is scorching in the desert sun and surrounded by brown, choking smog. Hot summers have long been recognized as contributory factors in urban unrest and East LA certainly has hot ones.

By contrast, no part of the city of San Diego is more than ten miles from the ocean and the oldest barrio, Logan Heights, is right on San Diego Bay. So the kind of miserable breathing conditions which people suffer with in LA do not exist in San Diego.

Nonetheless, the San Diego police department lists about thirty-five gangs within the city, another fifteen in the rest of the county. The neighboring city of National City alone accounts for seven in the latter group. Of course these numbers fluctuate as gangs rise and fall in activity.

Many of my friends in San Diego's barrios say to me, "We don't have gangs here; we have neighborhoods. Those dudes up in LA are crazy, real *vatos locos*; we're not rowdy like that." I agree. San Diego is relatively peaceful. But even if people on the streets do not see themselves as gang members, they may fit into the definition the police use.

Sergeant Bill Campbell is head of the Gang Detail for the SDPD. He enumerates four criteria by which his ten investigative detectives determine whether or not a youth is in a gang: does he have a name for his group, do they claim a certain region as their territory, do the members associate together frequently, and do they engage in criminal activity?

There are two main written forms of claiming gang affiliation: tattoos and graffiti. Among the Mexican-American gangs which, according to Sgt. Campbell, amount to about two-thirds of the total number of San Diego gangs, the graffiti are called *placas* or *placasos*. A *placa* generally consists of simply two elements, the street nickname of the person writing and the initials of his or her barrio.

"Girls are sometimes part of the gang," says Sgt. Campbell, "but mostly in an associate capacity, not usually involved in hardcore criminal activity."

The SDPD has a card file of two thousand youths whom they call gang members.

In junior high and high school it is quite trendy for Chicano youths to go to school dressed in baggy pants very neatly ironed, shiny black shoes, and wearing either a plain white T-shirt or a shirt of some unique sort, worn in a very macho manner, often with long tails hanging out. This is called *cholo* garb and derives from the gang style of dress though not all who wear it are gang members. Part of the style is to walk with a rigid, forward look, no smile, chin lifted in a stare of defiance. All of this is sure to cause other people to yield place on the sidewalk and to gain the attention of any passing police. So any youth who dresses like a *cholo* falls into suspicion of being a gang member.

The Mexican-American gang members of the 1940s and '50s called themselves *pachucos* and they developed the zoot-suit style of dress. Today's *cholo* is an evolutionary development from the *pachuco*. "My father was a *chuco*, but I'm a *cholo*."

And so it is about the *cholo* homeboy that I write and I do so for many reasons. Though I myself am an Anglo and a college teacher, I have long admired the creative artistry which is expressed in the *cholo* lifestyle. They are just as gutsy in standing up for their unique mode of living as were the hippies or anyone else who wore long hair in the face of the short hair of the establishment. They are beautiful, intelligent people and there is no reason why they should not take their own place in American society.

Though the *cholo* is descended from Mexican ancestry, though he cherishes that origin, he has given rise to a unique and inventive part of a truly American society. The *cholo* is as American as jazz. He would be entirely out of place in Guadalajara, but in the United States of America he flourishes like the cedars of Lebanon.

Criminal activity, of course, I have never admired, but today's homeboy is stepping above that, is developing his potential in whatever positive way he can muster. College is not for everyone, but many homeboys are recognizing that the community college system offers them vast possibilities for self-fulfillment. With pride in *La Raza* (their race) as well as in themselves, they say, "Hey, man, I wanna live; I am going to live—another forty, fifty, even sixty more years. I have time to make something of myself and I can, yes, I can! *Si se puede!*"

The stories in this book are true life. Like life, they are not all roses. No one can expect to succeed one hundred percent of the time. Let's say, for example, that I succeed ten percent of the time. That means that out of every ten attempts, I will have success one time. Now if I try only ten things in life, I will succeed in only one. If I stop there, that one accomplishment may be my only success in life, but if I go on and attempt ten more things, what do you think? I will have one more positive effect. No one ever gets anywhere without trying. So the more things we try, the more we will succeed in.

Thus, dear reader, I am sure you can do whatever you want badly enough. I know you can, but do you know it? You have a purpose in life. Only you can find it. Wake up each morning and go searching for the goodness which is inside of you.

The ancient philosophers speak of the transcendentals: goodness, truth, beauty, and unity. They say that the transcendentals are interchangeable, meaning that anything which is good is also true, beautiful, and has a certain unity. This interchangeability works in all combinations. Thus, as another example, that which is true is also beautiful, is also good, and has a certain unified character that holds it together to be what it is.

Applying these thoughts to ourselves, note that we are in existence. That is a truth: you exist. Now, according to the theory of the transcendentals, the truth of your existence is also beautiful. You are beautiful! You are also good and you have a certain unity. So you are true, beautiful, good and unified.

Try this theory on anything. Look at a beautiful girl. Isn't that beauty good? That's true. And when we say some current expression like, "She's got it all together," or "Wow, is she ever stacked," we are affirming her unity, her togetherness. So the transcendentals work on everything.

Similarly, when you go to school, everything you learn is a truth. Cherish it! For that which is true is also beautiful and good and unified with a unique existence which makes it stand on its own as a marvelous bit of creation. Be grateful for it and keep on going back for more until someday you will find yourself so full of goodness and truth that you will step out into your barrio and spread it to others. For that is all that life is, finding truth and recognizing its goodness and passing it on to your homeboy or your *ruca* (girlfriend), to all the people you can reach.

It's like when you're drinking beer and toking weed on Saturday night and you get all high and you pass the reefer to your homeboy and you throw your arm around his shoulder and you say, "Wow, homes, this is bad stuff; take a drag." That feeling of exhilaration, that rush you get, is nothing compared to the thrill you will get when you can turn your homeboys onto something really good for them, something like a fine education which will get them a good job and make them self-sufficient and able to support their favorite "old lady" and their own child.

And then, with the power which comes from education and the beauty of the truth you get there, you will raise your head up high in your barrio and you will say, "Come on, homies, this is the best darn barrio there ever was and we have the power to make it even better."

I don't know what you will do with this power and this truth, but you will know, you will see what to do. For the beauty of education is that it gives you alternatives; it gives you different paths you can choose, different things you can do. So one morning you will wake up and you will say, "Hey, homes, this is what we're going to do today." And you'll go out that day and do one good thing, as if you were laying a brick for a wall. And the next morning you will jump out of bed and grab a whole armload of bricks and you will shout, "Come on, *compadres*, let's get this thing going; we can build a whole wall today." And you will stack one truth upon another and you will use that fantastic strength and beauty which is inside of you and you will gush over the whole neighborhood and spread out into the city and your creativity will be manifest to all the world. For, indeed, you can; *si su puede*! Yes, you can—and you will.

Turn now to the stories in this book as examples of what homeboys have done and of what you can do. Look at the positive aspects of each story and take off from there. All of life has negative things as well as positive ones, but we cannot let the negative ones rule and guide our lives.

For example, everyone dies. The end of every life story is death. But we do not say, "What the heck, I'm going to die so why should I bother to do anything?" No. We look at what good things we can do and we focus our attention on the positive side of life. So, please, dear reader, think of these stories in that way.

Hilario, *El Professor*
Hilary Paul McGuire
San Diego City College

1 CHANGO, TOPO, AND SMILEY, STARTERS OF A DECADE

"Hi, guys," I said as I approached three grim-looking *cholos* out front of my apartment, "have you seen this book?"

"Naw, man, we don't wanna see no book," scowled the guy on the left. He turned his head away with a look of disdain as if he wanted to add, "How dare you speak to us; don't you know we're hard dudes, man?"

Unabashed, I persisted, but this time thrust the book into the hands of the middle *vato* saying, "It's about East LA and it has pictures."

Immediately the three young men were looking over each other's shoulders, paging through the little paperback, and making comments about the pictures.

"Hey, that dude looks like Smokey," and, "There's a *vato* I knew in CYA (California Youth Authority detention center)."

I was looking too, so when they pointed to one photo, I said, "That guy was a very close friend of mine, but he's dead now."

"Yeah," said the young man holding the book, "those *vatos* in LA are crazy. How'd he die?" As he spoke, he shut the book and handed it back to me.

"A guy from a rival gang stabbed him in the back with a broken beer bottle," I replied. Then I offered the book *Hopie and the Los Homes Gang* to the third youth saying, "I wrote this book."

"Yeah, man?" he said, giving me a disbelieving look in the face.

"Yes," I replied gently, "my picture's on page 27."

The book-holder flipped to page 27, looked hard at the picture, then glanced up at me to confirm my identity. Still doubtful, he said, "Do you know these dudes?"

"Sure," I asserted, "this whole book is about our experiences together."

By this time the first guy who had turned down the book wanted another chance at it. So he reached for it and took control.

Now that I had broken the ice with these fellows who would never have spoken to me otherwise, I pursued my opening. "You guys go to school over here?" I motioned toward San Diego High School across the street diagonally.

"Naw, man, we got suspended."

"When did they suspend you?"

"Last year."

"And you haven't been back since?"

"Naw. They don't want us."

Only one fellow seemed to be doing any talking. The others were still poring over the book. "*Yo soy* Hilario (My name is Hilary)," I said as I stuck out my hand to shake with him.

He gave my hand the complicated slipping and clamping handshake current on the streets, grinned broadly, and said, "I'm Smiley." He poked his elbow at the fellow next to him saying, "This is Topo and that's Chango."

I knew that Chango meant monkey, but the other word escaped me. So I queried saying, "Topo? What does Topo mean?"

"Ground squirrel," interjected Topo, the largest and huskiest of the three. I was reminded of how ironic street names can be. Sometimes they fit perfectly, as did Smiley's name, while other times they can be very opposite, almost tongue-in-cheek, as in the case of Topo who looked more like a grizzly bear than a ground squirrel.

"How old are you guys?" I asked with a purpose in mind.

Smiley said, "Twenty," and Topo responded for the other two, "I'm nineteen and so is Chango."

Chango was still eyeing me suspiciously. "Well, hey," I said lightly, "I teach over here at City College and I happen to know that you can get into college without even having a high school diploma."

I half expected to receive a gruff "So what?" but Smiley made a very positive come-back. "Oh yeah? Do they have welding over there?"

"Sure. They've got everything."

"I've been thinking about getting a training," Smiley continued. "Do you know where we go to get signed up?"

"Sure. I could take you over there right now, introduce you to some people."

"Do they have some kind of financial aid?"

"You bet. In fact I know this real cool dude named Cruz Rangel and I'm sure he can help us."

"Let's go, homeboys," Smiley said.

Just then, while we were waiting for the light to cross over to San Diego City College, the three spotted another homie. So we waited for him and that's how I met Diablo. They explained to him where we were going and he trudged right along with us, swinging his long arms straight down at his side and saying, "My old man's been telling me I ought to get a training."

We turned quite a few heads as we sauntered across campus. Though San Diego High is right next door to City College and dozens of young *cholos* come on campus daily to get lunch at the college cafeteria, there was something much more sinister about these older fellows. By this time I had been teaching there for three years and I had never seen a homeboy on campus for college classes. That had always struck me as peculiar since daily a couple hundred high school students dressed as *cholos* and *cholas* passed right by the college on their way to and from home.

We went in to see Mr. Cruz Rangel, then director of the EOPS Program (Extended Opportunity Programs and Services). He was familiar with my book and my work in East Los Angeles so he was very cooperative. "You guys been out of school for a while, eh?"

The EOPS director proceeded to outline some of the many possibilities available on campus. "We offer several forms of financial aid," he began. "There are four types of grants and two kinds of loans."

I interrupted to explain, "A grant is pure money, free and clear, but a loan is money you'll have to pay back a few years after you get out of school and get a job."

Rangel's office was decorated in such a way as to make Mexican-American students feel comfortable. He had a basketball-sized Aztec head of some sort sitting on the corner of his desk. On the wall hung a Mexican flag and across the back of the visitor chair where Diablo was sitting was a colorful Mexican blanket. Rangel himself was wearing a shirt of obvious Latin design. He toyed with a letter opener as he continued in his casual drawl. "For all of these aid packages, you apply with just one form; we call it the SAAC, Student Aid Application for California. If you qualify for help according to the standards which are in effect, we can set you up with some grant money, maybe some loan, and a work-study job on campus." He looked Chango full in the face and said, "Do you want a job?"

Chango, from whom I'd scarcely heard a syllable so far, shuffled his feet, looked down at his hands on his lap, and mumbled, "Sure, man, that's what we're here for."

So the director went on, "The work-study program gives you a job on campus at times when you're not in class. You might be working in the library or helping a particular instructor." Rangel was reading the eyes of my new friends and those prospects did not seem to interest them so he tried some other choices. "There are also jobs with non-profit corporations like the Boys' Club and the YMCA if you prefer an off-campus placement. On campus maybe you'd like working with the gardening department or the custodial staff or doing some kind of maintenance."

The atmosphere was getting pretty heavy, I thought, too many big words and too many choices to make might be discouraging to my friends. So I said, "Well, guys, you can see that there are lots of possibilities and we're here to help you get into whatever is right for you. Do you think you'd like to fill out an application?"

Chango, Topo, Smiley, and Diablo all nodded their heads in affirmation so Rangel stood up and stepped over to a book shelf where there were stacks of papers. "Here you go," he said, "you each take one of these and if you have any trouble filling them out, we have counselors who will give you a hand—or maybe Mr. McGuire here will help you."

"Sure," I said, "that's what I'm here for."

We spent the whole afternoon visiting with counselors, filling out forms, and picking through the class schedule trying to find welding classes which were still open. It certainly was a bewildering bunch of red tape, I realized, and it was not over yet. We learned that part of the forms had to be filled out by their parents using their last year's income tax form.

I apologized to them, "Sorry, guys, I didn't know this was going to be so complicated."

But the young men were very patient and Smiley replied, "That's alright; we can handle it."

They went home promising to return tomorrow.

The next day I ran into Chango and Smiley sitting on

Photo 1 - Smiley, Diablo, Chango, and Topo
Photo by Robert Estrada, Vietnam Vet and college student

the big stone wall which bears the name of the college. "Where are the other guys?" I asked.

"At home."

"Did you finish filling out the papers?"

"Naaa, my father didn't get around to it," replied Smiley.

"What about yours?" I asked, turning to Chango.

"I lost mine."

That was discouraging, but nothing like a piece of information I had discovered on campus that day. "We need welding equipment," I informed them. "Do you know of anyone who has a welding helmet?

Both Chango and Smiley shook their heads dejectedly.

"Well, I have a friend who teaches welding; let's go talk to him and see if we really need all that stuff."

So we went over to the welding shop where we found Mr. Denis Horn. He was wearing a leather jacket and a big pair of leather gloves as he spoke. "They certainly do need equipment, about one hundred dollars' worth. They gotta have goggles and helmet and gloves and jacket and a sparker." He looked at us with sympathy for our plight. "How many guys you got?" he asked.

"Four," I replied.

"I'll tell you what I'm gonna do," said Horn, "I have some special sources. You go ahead and get the guys enrolled and I'll see what I can do."

We never knew where he got the equipment, but soon after school started, we had enough of everything for all four homeboys. Even though the youngsters were not accustomed to expressions of gratitude, I thanked Mr. Horn profusely.

There is more to getting financial aid than just taking one welding class. If the homies wanted full aid, they had to take a full schedule of classes. So they signed up for an English class, a Chicano Studies class, and for a math class which I was teaching. I had made sure they would all be with kind teachers who would give them whatever special encouragement might be needed.

I sometimes went by their classrooms to check on their progress. One time I arrived after the class had been dismissed. But I could tell that my friends had been there because their names were on the blackboard in typical gang graffiti style:

CHANGO
L–TOPO–Hts
SMILEY

The LHts was an indication of their neighborhood, Logan Heights, the oldest barrio in San Diego.

From the start they did not attend my math class very regularly. When they came, they marched boldly to the front of the class to take seats five, ten, or fifteen minutes late. Unfortunately the class I was teaching was not the ideal one for them. They should have been in college arithmetic, a sort of pre-algebra class, but I was not teaching that this semester. They didn't care what I was teaching; if they had to take math, they preferred the class I was teaching and I supposed that I would be able to help them through with outside tutoring sessions.

It did not work out that way. Diablo hardly ever showed up. Never was there a time when all four came. Math is the kind of class that requires regular attendance.

Each day builds on the previous session. So I was immediately scrambling to give them enough tutoring.

One day I had seven homeboys in my office at one time. Don't ask me where they all came from. Some were other friends of my homies, just hanging around on the street corner when I invited my friends in for a tutoring session. They were all very well-behaved. Some sat on the floor, others lounged in chairs or on desks while I explained some theory of mathematics involving exponents.

I was sharing the office with another teacher. We shall call him Mr. Gorman. He had an extensive library of books against one wall of the room. While I was teaching math, Diablo apparently spotted a nice dictionary among the books.

As we were finishing the session, Diablo pulled the dictionary from the shelf saying, "Hey, Hilario, let me take this."

"What for?" I asked.

"I need it for English class."

"That's Mr. Gorman's book," I objected.

"I'll just borrow it for a few days," Diablo contended. "Gorman won't miss it."

I thought that was pretty good reasoning (I had never seen Gorman use the book), so I gave my approval. I was proud of Diablo for recognizing an academic need and providing for it.

As the weeks went by, the homeboys decided that they really only wanted to stay with welding. The amount of money provided by the financial aid people was not enough to inspire them to attend the other

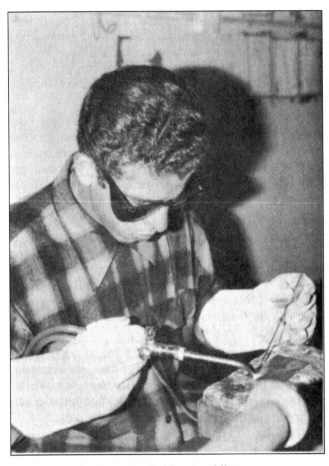

Photo 2 - Diablo at welding
Photo by Robert Estrada

classes. So they dropped math, English, and Chicano Studies and kept going to welding. The welding instructor Mr. Anaya was quite pleased with their work. Each one of them was working at a separate table doing individual work.

Another pleasant advance came when Mr. Horn announced that we could keep all the welding equipment. Each of the guys had an equipment locker and this donation released me from having to worry about keeping track of those materials.

Several weeks later my officemate Gorman missed his dictionary. When I told him that one of my friends had borrowed it, he flew at my throat, "You let those thugs come into my office? How dare you? Don't you know that you can't trust those animals as far as you can throw them?"

Calmly I tried to explain to him that I had a perfect right to see my students in my office and that they had all acted as perfect gentlemen.

"Perfect gentlemen, my foot," retorted Gorman. "Does a gentleman steal a book in an office which is not his?"

"He didn't steal it," I assured him. "He asked me quite properly if he might borrow it and I thought it'd be OK, that you wouldn't even miss the book for a while."

Gorman stood up to his full dictatorial height and reiterated, "You can't change those punks; once a punk, always a punk. It makes me sick to see people like you trying to be do-gooders."

I did not want to anger Mr. Gorman, for he was my senior on the faculty and quite an influential fellow, but I did want him to understand my position. "I believe that people act the way we expect them to act," I said gently. "If you treat someone with disdain, he will respond to you in like manner."

"Don't give me any of that goodie-goodie bullshit," shouted Gorman. His giant hulk was pacing back and forth from his desk to mine. "I want that dictionary back and I want it soon; and don't let those thugs into this office again unless I'm here."

"OK," I said, "I'll call Diablo tonight and if he doesn't have the book I'll buy you a new one."

"Diablo?" shouted Gorman, "That means Devil doesn't it? Do you mean to say that you hang around with a thug who calls himself the Devil?"

"I don't hang around with him," I retorted, "I just try to help him get an education."

"Well, the first lesson you should have taught him was to keep his paws off my stuff." Enough said, Gorman stomped out of the room, slamming the door behind him.

Luckily, I thought to myself, there are very few teachers at City College with an attitude like Gorman's. Most are like Anaya, Rangel, or Horn. In the counseling department there are people who will bend over backward to help those who need help with complicated paperwork or who will guide students into appropriate classes with teachers suited to their particular needs and temperament.

When I asked Diablo about the dictionary, he promised to bring it to welding class with him. By this time he had dropped English, so would not be needing the dictionary. But when I saw him on campus, he said, "What? Oh, the dictionary. I forgot it." That's the way it always went and so finally I had to buy a new dictionary for Mr. Gorman.

Of course Gorman took that opportunity to tell me, "I told you so."

But I try never to look at the negative side. I figured that wherever that book might be, even if Diablo had sold it to a hock shop, it was probably doing as much good as it would for Gorman. After all, that dictionary did not carry an adequate definition of "redneck." All it said was "an uneducated, white farm laborer," not at all descriptive of Mr. Gorman.

As a teacher I had occasion to carry various pieces of audio-visual equipment across campus. One day I was carrying a loudspeaker system with me when the homeboys joined me for the walk. Topo wanted to carry the speaker for me so I allowed him to. With his big, bearish frame moving beside me and the other guys ahead and behind, I looked like I was flanked by bodyguards. To make the scene even more amusing, Topo put the battery-powered microphone to his lips and, with a low amplification of his gruff voice, said, "Logan Heights." The speaker which he carried in his hand spoke out from the midst of our group, not loudly, but with calm proclamation, "Logan Heights, Logan Rules, Logan is Number One." Thus did Topo take advantage of just one more opportunity to spread the name and fame of his barrio.

Of course the usual way to announce their presence was to use graffiti. During the few days when the *cholos* attended my math class, they almost always left me a paper after class showing the gang-style doodling they had done when I thought they were taking class notes.

One such offering said, "Logan Heights Big Crazy Gang." They use the word crazy because they're proud to be thought of as crazy. Another common practice is to list several gang members by nickname and, after the list, write "*Locotes*," a street slang variation of "*locos*" (crazies).

I would like to suggest, however, that these young men are no more crazy than the rest of humanity who devise whatever monuments they can to mark their passage through the world. It is a normal, human desire to want to leave a mark on the world. Some people have made pyramids and tall buildings or monumental sculptures like the Eiffel Tower or the Watts Towers. Others pursue landmark law cases or perform actions which are recorded in history. Almost everyone makes babies in a conscious or unconscious effort to pass life and personal philosophy on to future generations.

Graffiti is as ancient as recorded history. The cavemen left marks on their caves. Toilet stalls even have the power to immortalize humans, if someone would care to preserve a bathroom wall.

So homeboys are not crazy by reason of their graffiti. In fact *cholo* graffiti is far more beautiful and artistic than most graffiti in history. That is what makes it remarkable. It may endure and develop as an art form.

However, most graffiti is a low level form of human immortalization. Does most graffiti have any purpose more important than self-gratification? Building a beautiful car or doing something else which is an improvement of the world or an inspiration to the spirits of other human beings is a much more valid form of self-expression.

Photo 3 - Graffiti art by Smiley
done as doodling in math class and given to author after class

Like Smiley had said the first day I met him, "We want to make something of ourselves." As welders they would be able to leave their mark on the world by contributing to the construction of ships and buildings. I knew this was in the back of my friends' minds, but I never discussed it with them. I never preached at them or criticized them for writing their graffiti on the buildings across the street from the college. My purpose was to offer them something better, a better way to leave their mark in life. They never wrote on any of the college buildings; they just wrote with chalk on the blackboards or with ink or pencil on paper.

About seven weeks after the start of the semester, I visited the homeboys in the welding lab. All four of them were there working in individual booths like telephone booths with a canvas drape hung at the doors. I asked Mr. Anaya how they were doing and he was effusive with his praise, "They're all doing fine," he said, "but Diablo is definitely the best, very highly motivated and with good manual dexterity and coordination."

I went over to the booths and peeked into each one where my friends were working. Their project on this particular day was to learn to make straight lay-downs of a welding rod onto a slab of bare metal. Each young man welcomed me in a different way, but all with great exuberance. Chango shook my hand vigorously saying, "Aaaa, Hilario, *que paso*, what's happening, man?" He proudly showed me his work and explained what his purpose was.

They were about to quit for the day so they asked me to wait while they swept up around their booths, put their equipment into their lockers, and changed clothes.

Photo 4 - Graffiti on a building near campus

I stood watching them while continuing to quiz Mr. Anaya.

"Do they all have the skills to be good welders?" I asked him.

"Sure, almost anyone with normal physical ability can become a good welder with enough practice. But it's just like anything else, practice makes perfect. If you don't have the desire and persistence and you don't practice, you'll never do anything."

Soon the homeboys had changed into their street clothes and out of the dirty shirts full of holes from bits of flying, hot metal. They gingerly donned their *cholo*-style, spotless white T-shirts, careful not to touch them with dirty fingers or brush them against any greasy equipment.

Then we were off, headed across campus. I had to stop at the duplicating room to get some papers so my homies stepped in with me.

One of the campus security officers happened to be present and he at once started checking out my friends with a dirty look. Chango, Topo, Smiley, and Diablo, immediately took offense. They seemed to bristle like a short-haired dog does when he gets mad.

Luckily we had to spend only about forty-five seconds in that room, but as we walked away, I sensed a complete change of attitude from the very high spirits they had exhibited in the welding lab only minutes ago.

'Psss, *puerco*, *el* piggo," they hissed, hooted, and snorted as we walked away. They made grunting sounds like a rooting pig.

"Take it easy, guys," I said soothingly, "he just doesn't know what good people you are."

Smiley threw back his shoulders, raised his chin in a typical *cholo* gesture of defiance, and spat back at me, "We're not good people; we are bad dudes." He glared sullenly straight ahead and the others gave silent assent.

They were not at all the civilized young men that I had come to know. As we crossed campus, it was as if the mere sight of that security officer had transformed them into some kind of predatory animals. They swaggered along, hanging their arms rigidly from taut shoulder muscles.

"Wheeea-wheet!" they whistled at every pretty girl with the sort of whistle one would use to summon a dog.

Diablo made a suction with his lips to produce a bubbly, hissing sort of sound like lovers make with a loud kiss. People were looking at us from every side and I was for the first time uncomfortable with my friends who seemed to have undergone some personality change.

I didn't say anything, just hoped this phase would pass and my friends would be back to normal by tomorrow.

What went through their minds after I left them that day, we will never know. Did they forget the incident with the officer or did it fester in their minds, causing a rise in tension with the whole campus society? I am inclined to think they forgot it. My impression is that they do not ponder such insignificant matters. Yet my experience with gang members teaches me that very minor instances of violation of a member's honor can lead to violence and death.

At any rate, on the following day, when I ran into Mr. Anaya and casually asked if the guys had come to class, he replied, "Oh, yes, they were all there today except for Diablo."

I did not think that important since it was quite common for one or another of them to miss class, but later in the day I received the shock of the semester.

A phone call from the security office on campus reached me at my apartment across the street. "Mr. McGuire, would you please come over to the office right away; we want to ask you some questions about those young men we saw you with yesterday."

When I arrived at the office, to my great surprise, there on the bulletin board was a photostatic copy of a newspaper article about the homeboys and me. In the middle of the article was a very clear picture of all of us with an arrow, obviously drawn by one of the officers, pointing right at Diablo.

At that time I was still making radio and TV appearances in connection with my book *Hopie and the Los Homes Gang* and this particular article in the National City *Star News* of March 6, 1980 was a sort of follow-up to see what lessons I had learned in my Los Angeles work might be applicable to San Diego. I was deeply disturbed that now the police were going to use it to incriminate one of my students.

"What's the name of the guy with the arrow pointing at him?" queried one of the officers.

I felt myself in a tight spot. I did not want to jeopardize the future of the best welding student, and yet I was duty-bound to cooperate with legitimate authority.

"Diablo," I said, hoping that giving a non-specific nickname might be all I would need to do.

Photo 5 - Smiley, Topo, Diablo, Chango, and the author
Photo by National City *Star News*, March 6, 1980

"What's his complete real name?" they asked patiently.

"Why? What'd he do?"

"He and another fellow were spotted using a bolt cutter to cut the chain and steal a moped just an hour ago," said the security boss.

Quick work by the officers, I thought. It was beginning to appear that I would be forced to give Diablo's real name.

"But how do you know it was Diablo?" I persisted wanting to be sure they had the right man.

"A student saw them pull a long-handled bolt cutter from the bushes near the bike stands. He watched them start cutting the chain of the moped and he ran looking for security. Officer Rodriguez just happened to be near there in the college pickup truck. He got to the scene immediately and saw two guys jump onto the moped and start riding away carrying the bolt cutters. He chased them in the pickup and finally caught up to them about five blocks away, down on J Street."

"Wow," I interjected, "they got pretty far."

"Yes, but at that point Officer Rodriguez tried to apprehend the guy who was driving. Your boy Diablo was riding on the back. He slipped off the back and ran away while Officer Rodriguez was trying to cuff the driver. But the driver slipped away and started beating on Officer Rodriguez. Then he ran away leaving the moped behind."

"We've got them both for grand theft and the driver for battery on an officer," added another officer. "Now what is that dude's name? Officer Rodriguez has positively identified him in that picture."

So I reluctantly gave Diablo's real name, figuring I'd be cited for complicity if I didn't.

The head of security stepped over to me and said, "Mr. McGuire, we have already turned this matter over to the San Diego PD and they are already putting out an all-points bulletin based on this picture. Your best move would be to contact this student and get him to turn himself in."

I promised I would try to reach Diablo. As I left the security office, my head was reeling. Not much more than twenty-four hours ago I had received such a glowing report about Diablo's welding from his teacher. Now this. Would it end his college career? Would it affect the other homeboys?

Back at my apartment I dug out the list of phone numbers I had collected in case I needed to contact one of my friends. I tried Diablo's number. It was disconnected. So I called Smiley. He said the whole moped story was news to him and that he would try to contact Diablo with the idea of turning himself in.

After my evening class, I called Smiley's place again. Diablo was there and came to the phone. "I didn't have nothin' to do with that moped," he claimed. "I just barely met that guy this afternoon. He's a *vato* from Diego High and he told me he'd give me a ride home so I hopped on."

"Well, you'd better come and tell that to the cops because they have an APB out for you and it'll go hard for you if they catch you."

"Naw, man, I ain't gonna turn myself in; they won't believe me."

"If you don't, they'll come and find you."

"Naw, they'll never find me in my neighborhood."

"But," I argued, "if you don't get this thing fixed, you won't be able to come back to welding class."

Diablo grunted a regretful little grunt, but then he wrote off this whole career opportunity with a laconic statement, "That's OK, man."

There was a silence following that. I had a feeling it was the last word, but I tried arguing a bit more. "Get this thing settled; then you can come back and continue your welding. You're doing so well. Mr. Anaya says you're the best of all the guys."

"Naw, man. A few years and they'll forget my face; then I'll come back."

So that was it. I could do no more. I called the security office and reported my efforts.

The responding officer said, "OK, just forget it; we'll follow our regular procedures, turn the case over to criminal court."

Diablo never came back to class. He stayed in his barrio and never was caught. He has phoned me several times during the three years since then. At first he was just checking with me to see how the investigation was going. I suggested again that he might want to turn himself in and get a new start at welding someday, but he made a short refusal, just saying "Naw," with confidence that he would never be caught.

After about a year and a half, Diablo made some effort to get back into a welding class. By then he had a wife and child and he wanted a welding career. He called me and arranged to meet on the street so I could re-introduce him on campus. His face had been forgotten by then and the security officers were all different so I figured he had a good chance. But for one personal reason or another, my friend Diablo has never followed through, never completed the registration process—yet.

But life is long and this college or another source of training is always waiting for him. All it takes is time and desire and perseverance. For years the community college system had been free. It will, hopefully, always be inexpensive. And I am sure there will always be good people who will help a young person (or even a not-so-young person) to get a new start. Desire and good will and personal effort, when coupled with persistence and stick-to-it-iveness have always been triumphant for free human beings.

What about Chango, Topo, and Smiley? Though Diablo had been the best welder of the bunch, I came to learn in the next few weeks that each of the other homeboys had special talents.

Chango, the most silent and expressionless of the three, turned out to be unusually artistic and creative. I would never have learned that except that the day following the moped theft, the three went with me for another newspaper interview. The interviewer asked the young men for examples of their graffiti. Each one was to write on a piece of paper without looking at the work of the others.

Chango came up with the most unique work. He listed several of the homeboys from his neighborhood, then identified the barrio with ornate lettering "EAL's C 30." I knew that the C 30 meant "Calle Trienta," for Thirtieth Street, a subsection of Barrio Logan, but I had never seen "EA" before. We asked Chango what it meant.

He replied with typical brevity, "Ele Ache."

"What's that?" asked our interviewer.

"Spanish letters," Chango explained, "Those are the letters for LH."

Then I remembered, so I continued for the interviewer. "In Spanish there is a spelling for the letters of the alphabet like there would be if we would spell the letter B with the word 'Bee' or the letter Q with 'Cue.' So *'ele'* is the way they spell and pronounce the letter L (pronounced el-ay) and *'ache'* is the spelling and pronunciation of the letter H (pronounced ah-chay). *Ele Ache* therefore stands for Logan Heights. And of course 'L's' after the EA means *locos* or *locotes*."

The interviewer was fascinated. He used Chango's graffiti in his article. And I knew my enigmatic friend Chango just a little better.

Smiley had always stood out as the most talkative and affable member of this group and newspaper interviews were no exception. Any question which was put to the group was answered by Smiley, as if being spokesman was his official duty. The only way the interviewer could get a word out of Chango or Topo was to make a direct question for them.

Smiley said that both he and Topo are the youngest of families of eleven children each, both families having eight boys and three girls, and that they live within a block of each other.

Smiley also told about the day he got shot in the hand. "I was walking with some girls and some *chavala* I didn't know pushed me. Later I heard that they were out to shoot me. One day when another *vato* and I were out walking, shots started coming our way. My homeboy had a piece so he started shooting back. I got hit in the hand."

The interviewer asked, "Did the shot break any bones

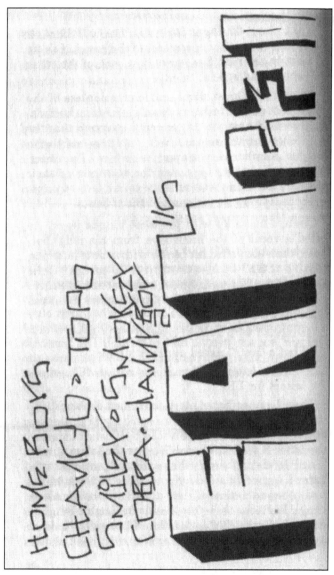

Photo 6 - Chango's artistry for news reporter

in your hand?"

"Naaa," Smiley replied shortly without offering to show his hand. Apparently it healed alright because Smiley shows no sign of deformity.

In my effort to help the homeboys get an education, I made a point of not asking too many personal questions because the guys might think I was getting too nosey and that might jeopardize our relationship. I would rather just offer them the value of education and let them tell me other things when they felt like doing so.

But the interviewer kept asking questions like, "What do you think of Mr. McGuire here?"

I was shocked and a bit embarrassed by the question.

But Smiley looked like it was an easier question than those about his past life. His face lightened up and he reached over to give me a big pat on the back as he said, "If it wasn't for him, we'd all be standing around doing nothing and being scolded by our parents for not getting a job."

From there we went outside for some photos and once again Chango came to the fore as the unofficial public information officer for the group. From his position crouching with me in front of Smiley and Topo, Chango made his hands form an LH. It dawned on me then that Chango, as the public relations man, was the one who always wrote the graffiti on the walls and that he always put his name on the top of the list of names he was making.

But if this group of *cholos* was living in a symbiotic relationship in which each member contributed to the welfare of the whole, what was the function of my friend Topo?

Topo was the cement and the corner post of the group. As the largest of all the youths, he was the stalwart backbone, perhaps even the bodyguard. His unsmiling, square jaw and broad shoulders were too formidable to be challenged. His presence said to rival groups, "Don't mess with us."

Yet I knew him as tender, sensitive, and affectionate, traits which I am sure make him very popular with the ladies even though I have never seen anyone but Smiley flanked by women. Topo has always been very cordial to me, shaking hands with the gentleness of a teddy bear and greeting me with "*Que onda,* Hilario?" his equivalent of "What's happening, man?"

Other than those few words and my perception of his presence, he might have been considered The Invisible Man. Yet he represented a significant portion of the cohesive force in my little band of collegiate homies.

The moped incident and the loss of Diablo were quite a blow to the group. Whereas they had been going regularly to class, they suddenly quit. I still saw them hanging out on the college lawn, but there was always one reason or another why they weren't going to welding that day. First excuse was that Chango had hurt his hand falling off a moped. That was the only indication that he might have been involved in the theft of other missing mopeds, but I never asked. It was as if campus life was a completely different existence from that back home in their neighborhood. Knowing that the workaday world on one's job usually is and usually should be totally divorced from personal problems at home, I gladly fostered this dichotomy.

Another day the homies were all dressed up, "all

Photo 7 - Smiley, Topo, the author, and Chango (forming "LH")
Photo by *Southern Cross* newspaper, April 10, 1980

choloed out like hard dudes," as one of the other students expressed it. When I asked if they were on their way to class, Smiley replied, "Naaa, we're gonna meet some girls."

When I ran into Mr. Anaya, he said, "I don't expect they'll ever come back to welding."

But then, just as suddenly as they had stopped, they started back to class. It was exactly one week after Diablo's departure.

Then came Easter vacation. I hated it. Just when my friends were getting back into the groove, this could put them out of the habit and they might never return to their welding. A whole week went by.

When vacation was over, I eagerly visited the welding shop, hoping the homeboys would return. Sure enough, there they were.

Chango was seriously going about his business at a welding table as Topo and Smiley took me outside to see Topo's newly-acquired car. It was a beat-up, ancient (1963 model, I guessed) Chevy convertible, but obviously of a style which the guys felt would make a fine low-rider. Indeed, the front end was sitting right down on the ground, like a tired beast panting for breath.

"Does the back go down also?" I asked.

"Sure," said Topo with a proud little half-grin as if he were being careful not to break his *cholo*-style grimness, "we go low and slow."

He motioned me around to the rear of the car and had me bend over so I could see the hydraulic shocks. Then he stepped to the driver's side of the car, reached inside the front window, and flicked a button. The car settled to the ground with a little thud. A final bullet had put a wounded animal out of its misery.

I involuntarily broke into a wide smile just as Smiley and Topo did. Topo was extremely proud of his acquisition. "Got it for only six hundred," he chortled.

"Looks like a pretty good deal," I suggested.

"Sure is," said Smiley. "We're gonna take it to the hops this weekend at Chicano Park. This'n'll jump higher than the coke bottles, might win a prize if we get some new batteries."

I knew he was referring to the trunkful of batteries which are used to power the "lifters." A car can really bounce high when it gains momentum from flipping the switch up and down.

There was a muffler lying forlornly on the street near the back of the car.

"What's this for?" I asked.

"That's my muffler," Topo reported. "The guys next door in the mechanics shop are going to put it on for me."

It tickled me that the guys had learned so well about the services of the college. Students are allowed to work on their own cars or those of their friends during mechanics classes. Apparently Topo had made a friend in the neighboring shop.

We turned to go back into the welding shop. Chango was still steadfastly concentrating on his work. With big tongs he grabbed the piece of metal he had just finished welding. He plunged it into a vat of water and there came a big hiss and lots of steam. Without even glancing up, Chango turned back to the welding table, serious as a judge.

"C'mon," Smiley chided him, "it's time to go home."

Without comment, sober-faced Chango turned off his welding torch, gathered his sparker and goggles, then set them down, grabbed a broom and started sweeping the floor.

"Just part of the job," grunted Chango.

I do not understand what happened in the coming weeks. Chango, Topo and Smiley seemed to have forgotten the loss of Diablo. They had total control of their welding class. They liked the teacher and he liked them.

Maybe it was all too easy and they lost interest—not challenging enough. Or maybe personal life just interfered too much in their campus lives. All I know is that their welding attendance became sporadic. First they all missed class one or two days. When they came back, Topo was missing.

"Topo had a car accident," Smiley said, "cut his face."

"Is he hurt badly?"

"Naaa, just a scratch."

"So why doesn't he come back to school?" I wondered.

"He doesn't want anyone to see him."

Another day Chango was gone. A couple days later he reappeared with his head shaven bald. He was wearing a dark blue stocking cap to hide it. These caps, referred to as "beanies," had been a common part of gang uniform for several years, but at this particular time Chango was the only one wearing one so he stood out.

I could tell that his hair was gone so I asked about it.

He looked like he didn't really want to talk about it, but he sullenly responded, "I got in jail in TJ."

"They did that to you in Tijuana?" I asked incredulously.

"Yes, they do it to everyone in the jail down there."

Then Chango clamped his jaw and never said what had transpired on that mysterious weekend.

For whatever reasons, Smiley was the only homeboy in the college on several occasions and it did not seem that he spent much time in class. When I saw him, he was always among a group of friends to whom he would introduce me.

Some of the homies had read my *Hopie* book and wondered when I would write one about San Diego.

"I think you guys should write the next book," I said. "You write the stories and I'll gather them and see if we can get them published."

"We'll write you some 'bad' stories," said girls like Flacca and Cricket, but I never received the proof.

Several of the guys also liked the idea, but only Smiley actually sat down, right there on the benches in front of the college, and wrote some of his life story. That he was able to do all of this amid the comings and goings of other homies is proof of his great communication skill and that he could do a whole lot more if he were in a more quiet setting.

Here are Smiley's own words with some slight editing.

"The first day I met Hilario, I was walking down to McDonald's and he asked me and my homeboys if we would like to go to college. He helped us to enroll in his class and get a training so we are making it good. He is a good friend of us. He helps us to stay out of trouble. Right now here is my homegirl Happy talking to my teacher from math.

"I'm from Logan Heights and I'm twenty years old. Before I came to college I used to go to San Diego High, but I got dropped out.

"I like to go party, go to school, and stay out of trouble. I'm the youngest in my house.

"Before I came here to Logan, I used to be from Sidro. I know a lot of homeboys from Sidro (the San Ysidro barrio) so when I go down there they don't fuck with me, like I don't fuck with nobody.

"I live in Calle 33. My homeboy Topo lives in the same block as I do. We go party every weekend. We know a lot of people from different barrios. Me and all the homeboys are always together in everything. Like every Sunday we go to Chicano Park.

"Before I came to Logan I heard about the *vatos locos* from Chicano Park and Los Chicos from Calle 30th Crazy Gang."

Even as he wrote, Smiley was trading banter with other homeboys and was introducing me to *vatos* named Casper and Joker and Silent and Oldie. Several were talking about taking classes in the fall at the college or starting right away with the EOPS Summer Readiness Program which pays people who start college in the summer. Already Wolf and Li'l Man and a couple of dudes both named Louie were signed up for it.

Others like Panther and Pirata were still only juniors in high school so I encouraged them to stick with it until they could graduate. That might sound like typical preachy teacher, but for some reason they all seemed to appreciate it.

I thanked God for every little sign of homeboys making progress. We had come a long way, I figured, this semester. It was already May, just a month till the end of the spring semester, 1980, and still the guys were hanging on in welding class and others were considering what college might offer for their lives.

The next day I saw Topo for the first time since his car accident. He had the imprint of a Coke bottle top (not the bottom) on his right cheek bone. He was not any more full of explanations than ever so I can only surmise that the car wreck threw him against someone who was holding a cola bottle. But that was almost two weeks ago now and the imprint was still visible. It must have been a rather sizable cut when it was new.

Anyway, Topo was back in welding class and Mr. Anaya seemed able to cope with such sporadic attendance. Not all teachers are so tolerant and in most classes, when you miss something, you are lost. Apparently Anaya allowed the homies to work at their own pace. In most academic subjects, that would be impossible. However, there is an Independent Learning Center at many colleges now, an audio-visual center where video tapes and computers allow the student to study most subjects on a self-paced basis. Most of the time that learning does not give class credit, but the ILC is very useful as an outside support when one is taking a class.

For example, if one were studying the algebra section about factoring, the Independent Learning Center would have a video tape or a computer program to aid the student. So the ILC is a good place to acquire self-paced knowledge for almost any course which is not as liberal as welding.

Chango's bald-shaven head developed another problem. The *policía* in Tijuana had also cracked his head open with some kind of blow. After a couple of weeks, that wound, instead of healing, started festering. It was full of puss.

The campus security officers had been watching Chango, Topo, and Smiley since the moped incident. One of the officers was a woman who took a sympathetic interest in the homeboys. When she saw Chango's head bulging with infection, she did a little nursing. She took him to the security office and put her first-aid kit to work. After piercing the wound to release the fluids, she disinfected the area with alcohol and covered it with a bandage.

When I commented on Chango's bandaged head, he just grunted, "One of the pigs let the puss out," but I suspect his gruff exterior covered a grateful heart.

Things never seemed to stop going wrong for Chango. The next day he came to class limping and with one bare foot.

"It ain't nothing," Chango muttered, but Smiley revealed that his friend had stepped on a nail.

None of this kept Chango from making at least irregular appearances at welding. It seems that the support of the little clique was just enough to pull him through. I doubt that any of them would have made it through the semester without the companionship of the others.

But make it they did, all the way to the end of the semester. No one was happier about it than I was. In fact the homeboys never did any celebrating that I know of. They just took the final test and disappeared. It was as if they thought nothing of their accomplishment.

They were the first *cholo*-dressed hard dudes to make it through a daytime college class in the three years I had been teaching at City College. More importantly, they had started a pattern for the 1980s. Chango, Topo, and Smiley had been so well known and well-liked among their fellow homies that the fact of their going to college encouraged others to try.

The names of Chango, Topo, and Smiley stood out amid the graffiti on the walls in the vicinity of the college. Their graffiti, though I cannot personally condone the petty vandalism which it represents, was bigger and bolder than that of anyone else. That made them a very visible entity among the two hundred or more *cholos* and *cholas* who visited the high school and college neighborhood daily.

Their accomplishment was duly recognized by many of the younger *vatos* so that hence forward going to college would be a viable alternative for the graduates of San Diego High and even for those who might have dropped out for one reason or another, but who, once they reached the age of eighteen, would know that college would always be available to them.

So here's to Chango, Topo, and Smiley, the start of something big!

In the years since then, those guys and I have kept in touch sporadically. Some are married and have babies. All have had various jobs, but never in welding. Messers Anaya and Horn tried to steer them toward welding opportunities at NASSCO (National Steel and Shipbuilding Company) or with the Navy. But they needed further welding courses and experience before they could land one of those good-paying jobs.

Chango, Topo, and Smiley talked about coming back for another welding class in the fall, but too much water went under the bridge during the summer. Somehow all their welding equipment vanished. I had wanted to keep the things at my apartment, but the fellows insisted on taking them home, never to be seen at college again.

Nonetheless Diablo and the other three have enjoyed a valuable experience which they will never forget and which will bear fruit in many ways—for themselves and others—in the 1980s and beyond.

Thanks be to Diablo, Chango, Topo, and Smiley. Their spirit and creative efforts are marching on.

2 THE BIGNESS OF LI'L MAN

My phone rang at 7 a.m.

"Hilary," the voice said, "get your ass out of bed."

I groggily responded, "Who's this?"

"It's Li'l Man, of course; who'd'ja think it was?"

"Oh," I said, slowly coming to my senses, "what-'cha up to?"

"Listen, man, I wanna get into that summer class. How much they paying?"

"Well, I don't know exactly," I said candidly. "It changes from time to time, but last I heard it was about four hundred dollars for the five-week summer session."

"That sounds OK by me," Li'l Man rejoined with a smack of his lips.

There was a pause and I wondered what my new friend was doing up so early. I did not have long to wonder. He continued.

"How's about meeting me somewhere and helping me with some of those papers?"

"Sure," I gladly agreed, "but I have class from 8 'til 9."

"That's cool; I'll meet'cha afterward. What room ya in?"

He met me later as promised, but had with him only half of the necessary papers.

"Where is your father's tax return from last year?" I asked. I had warned him that the EOPS program awards grants on the basis of family need and that he would have to prove that his father is not some big rich dude.

"Oh," he said, "I left that in my friend's car. I'll go get it and meet you right away at your apartment."

Since I lived across from the college, I went to my room, did some putzing around, then came out expecting to find Li'l Man.

No such luck. I went to breakfast, telling Topo to tell Li'l Man to join me at the restaurant.

I finished breakfast and headed home. Still no Li'l Man.

Hours passed. This was the last day to sign up for the program so I called Li'l Man's home. His mother answered in Spanish so I told her, "*Yo soy* Hilario, *el professor del colegio*," and gave my number.

I was soaking wet in the shower when Li'l Man finally called, not from home, but from the phone on the street downstairs. He sounded as if nothing had happened, as if I were an idiot to have been wondering where he was all day.

"I know how to play those silly games," I told myself, so I played it cool and just said, "I'm in the shower, be down in about fifteen."

"OK," he said, "I'll kick back at McDonald's 'til you come."

Of course when I came out, he was nowhere to be found. Across the street on the college lawn, I talked to some other *vatos*. No one had seen Li'l Man.

I was just about to go back to my room when Li'l Man came sauntering out of McDonald's, but looking like he was not seeing me. I had looked in McDonald's, but he had not been there. Familiar as I am with the swift appearance and disappearance of *cholos* on the street, I was not surprised. He could have been halfway to his barrio and back—half a dozen times.

Anyway, he came straight toward me, but looking rather groggy. To my amazement, he turned before he got to me and went toward the high school as if he had never seen me.

I could not believe it. I whistled and shouted his name, but he did not respond. Finally I ran after him.

Sure enough, he had not seen me, had forgotten entirely about our planned meeting, and I had a very sneaky suspicion that he had found a nickel bag of pot in his friend's car this morning and had been making friends all day by sharing it with others.

He was friendly and agreeable as ever, however, so he at once agreed to go with me to the EOPS office. He even had the needed tax papers tucked neatly inside his shirt.

The EOPS director personally helped us, approved of what Li'l Man had already done in filling out the forms, and gave a few helpful hints. He said that the classes would stress "survivor skills" for college, helping the student become familiar with the innumerable services and helpful personnel on campus: tutors, counselors, library, Independent Learning Center, financial aids, student nurse, enrollment procedures, et cetera, et cetera.

"Best of all," he said, "we have two hundred slots for this program and so far we have only one hundred people in it; so get out on the streets and tell your homeboys about it. We pay $410 for a five-week program, five hours per day, five days a week."

Today's deadline was not the final one so others would still have a chance to join. Li'l Man promised to spread the word. He is such an affable fellow that I had high hopes that he would find at least half a dozen stone *cholos* to take advantage of this offering.

As we walked back across campus, Li'l Man seemed even more talkative than Smiley.

"What'cha doin' this evenin', man?" he asked me. "I'm throwin' a little party over to my pad—gonna be plenty of reefer and mushroom. You oughta come by."

Though greatly flattered by the invitation I had to tactfully indicate a higher ideal.

"Well," I said with a slow drawl to give myself time to recover my wits, "I really wouldn't be interested in pot or peyote; I've tried pot briefly and don't like the way it messes with my mind. I like to be in complete control of myself."

"You're in control, man," he assured me, "just seein' pretty lights all around you."

"Yeah, but then you forget to do things like you forgot this morning that you'd promised me you'd be right back with your papers. Then you walked right past me on the street without recognizing me. You call that being in control?"

My friend smiled at me sheepishly. "Ah, well," he said with a wave of his hand, as if he were swatting flies, "I didn't have nothing important to do today anyway."

"Nothing important?" I squawked, "This chance to get started in college and get paid for it at the same time could be a major point in your whole life."

"Naaa, school is school, just a bunch of duddy teachers—don't know their ass from grass about life." Li'l Man put his head down and shook it as he spoke, simultaneously throwing both his hands up to shoulder height, bent at the elbows. I interpreted it as a gesture of utter disdain and it hurt me.

"Is that what you think of me?" I asked mournfully.

"Naaa, you're alright, man—just most of them."

"You'd be surprised," I said, "there are a lot of people better than I am if you just got to know them."

By this time we had reached the other side of campus. Having been filling out papers and visiting different offices most of the afternoon, I was getting hungry.

"You wanna get something to eat?" I asked.

We went to a quiet restaurant and sat down.

"All I want out of life," confided Li'l Man, waxing philosophical "is a car, a pad, a woman, some reefers, and a gun."

"Omigosh," I replied, "you sure do need an education; there's so much more to life than that. If you had all those things, you'd be bored as heck inside a year."

Silence fell between us for a few seconds. I wracked my brain for a way I could get through to this fine, intelligent, young man. He has so much potential, such vibrancy of life. It made me ache to want to open the doors of the world to him. I could not take him to the top of a high mountain and show him all the kingdoms of the world stretched out at his feet. I felt helpless to impart to him all the spiritual and intellectual dimensions of life. All I could point to was the one source of all these things for my own life—that boring-sounding thing called "education" and all the values it can provide. How could I lead him to that trough of knowledge and truth, that font of light and goodness? If I could just get him to trust me, I could take him by the hand and lead him all the way to the top of the tree…

But before I could think of what to say, Li'l Man broke in.

"Do you still have your cherry?" he asked casually.

I about dropped my teeth. Did he mean by this expression what I had learned from my *cholo* friends in East LA? They had referred to "popping a girl's cherry," meaning the act of releasing her from her bonds of maidenhood. Surely Li'l Man had a different meaning.

Skeptically I asked, "What's that? What do you mean?"

"You know, man," Li'l Man scowled impatiently, "Are you still a virgin?"

"No, I must admit," I stammered, "I'm not."

"Good," he said exuberantly, slapping the table with glee, "I'll invite you to some of our parties. We've got some fine weed that's guaranteed to make the girls as horny as hell."

"I don't know any horny girls," I rejoined, stretching the truth to indicate my lack of satisfaction with the ones I did know.

"Don't worry," Li'l Man purred, "we have plenty of them. I have stuff you buy for ten dollar a joint…"

I whistled. "Whew," I said, "that's big money; I never am dope enough to waste my money on such things."

"Nah, naaa," he chided, "what'cha do is break it down and roll yourself about ten small ones; they're plenty powerful and you get ten good lays for just ten bucks."

"That sounds a bit idyllic," I replied. "I don't trust things that are too good to be true and anyway, I don't care. I wouldn't waste my money on that stuff. I've never yet spent a cent on making myself dopey and I never will; I like the way my body is. Didn't you ever go running or play a hard game of football and come in and take a hot shower? You feel clean all through—like a million bucks. I wanna take good care of my body— keep a sound mind in a sound body as the philosophers say."

Li'l Man looked at me with bewilderment, as if either he did not know the feeling I referred to or thought I was crazy for preferring it to being high on dope.

"Aw, man," he groaned, "just forget it."

By that time we had finished eating. We had had enough meeting of the minds for one day. We went our separate ways.

Things were quiet for a few days. I was busy making out final exams, giving them, and making out grades. Then suddenly one morning I had a flood of homies. It was evident that Li'l Man was spreading the word.

I was going home from the college when I saw a couple of homeboys coming my way. Usually I would just dart across the street without waiting for the light, but one of the teens looked very much like Li'l Man. So I waited for the light to see if they wanted to talk to me. The short fellow was wearing a Pendleton shirt exactly like the one Li'l Man had been wearing when I last saw him. But as he came closer I could see it was not Li'l Man.

The light turned green and I almost started to cross, but to my surprise the young man with the Pendleton separated from the other one, headed straight toward me, and started speaking while still some distance away.

"Hey, where've you been; I've been looking for you."

In the past few months I had met so many of the dudes from San Diego High ("Day-go High" as they call it), thanks to the introductions of Smiley and my own friendliness, that I was embarrassed that I could not remember this guy's name.

"My friend from San Jose wants to get into that summer program," he continued. "We tried to call you, but you weren't home."

"I'm in and out all the time," I replied.

He took out his wallet and I could tell at once what an orderly fellow he was. He carefully opened the adhesive flap and I could see various photos plus the corner of a twenty dollar bill neatly folded with the corner showing. He dug deeper and pulled forth a folded piece of paper. As he unwrapped it, the names of several homeboys were showing, written in neat *cholo* script. There in one corner, in my own handwriting, was my name and phone number, offered to me now as evidence and a reminder that I had given this young man my promise that I would be available to help in any way I could.

I apologized for not being home all the time, but sought to remedy the error by saying, "Maybe we could call your friend right now, possibly get him enrolled today."

I fished a dime out of my pocket as we talked and soon we were on the phone talking to his friend Boxer.

My companion did the talking, "Boxer, this is Sharkey. Listen, man I've got that dude from the college here with me, the teacher. He says you should come right now, call him when you get here."

Boxer promised to be on his way. I thanked Sharkey for the introduction and he went on his way to high school classes.

Turning to go into my apartment, I was accosted by two other *vatos*.

"Hey, man," one of them said, "my *carnal* wants to get in on your program."

"The one that pays four hundred dollars?" I asked, getting ready to assure him that it was not my program, but one sponsored by the state.

"That's it," he replied. Then before I could make any explanation, he continued, "I'll give you his number; you call him, but don't tell him you saw me right now because I'm supposed to be in class."

He produced a graffiti marker from his pocket and, since we did not have a paper, proceeded to write in thick script on my hand the name and number of his close friend, his *carnal*.

"I guess Li'l Man told you about the Summer Readiness Program?" I asked.

"Yeah, and it sounds like a real good deal."

I assured him that it was and went to my room to use the phone to arrange to meet the new fellow. Then I stepped out again to eat breakfast at McDonald's.

There I saw a guy named Eddie and a *chola* named Lippy whom I had met recently. I asked if I could sit with them and they readily agreed.

As we sat there the girl was writing radio dedications of songs as if she planned to call some radio stations like XPRS in LA which plays lots of oldies and takes barrio dedications. When I started to eat, she was just beginning with a headline saying: "To All My Homeboys and Homegirls from Barrio LOGAN, *el Primero.*"

I went about my eating, chatting with her and Eddie while she continued to write.

About ten minutes later Eddie took the notebook from Lippy and started reading the names of the songs and the nicknames of the persons to whom each should be dedicated. To my utter amazement, Lippy had, in that short time, written down about three pages full of about fifty different dedications. I was shocked because even I, an experienced writer, would have difficulty putting ink to paper so rapidly.

Hoping to build on a good talent, I said, "You sure like to write."

Lippy muttered some sort of acknowledgement as the music from their large black portable radio with silver knobs droned on. The radio was the latest thing in music producers since palm-sized transistor radios had lost flavor due to their small amount of sound. This one could be heard a block away.

The music was too loud for calm conversation so I ate without speaking. Then suddenly, when a song finished, Eddie turned down the volume. He knew me from my *Hopie* book as a crusader for homeboy advancement, but I was not at all prepared for what he said out of the clear blue sky.

"I wish we'd all have a big party at the Chicano Federation," Eddie began, "and stop fighting each other."

Listening to the radio over a casual breakfast does not often give rise to such philosophical thinking, but the response which came from Lippy indicated conclusively that she was thinking on the same wave length and just as powerfully.

"I wish I could live to see the day," she said slowly.

I seized the opportunity to give them some suggestions based on their desires. "If you really want that," I said, "why don't you work for it. My theory is that if we don't try, we don't accomplish anything. In life we're lucky if we succeed fifty percent of the time. But that also means that the more things we try, the more success we will have. You might even use your talent for writing, Lippy. I've been thinking of coming out with another book, one about San Diego, but with stories written by the young people themselves. Maybe you can think of some way to write to encourage all the homeboys to live as homeboys of each other."

Lippy seemed to like the idea so I gave her my phone number so she could contact me with questions or finished product. Unfortunately, I have never heard from her since that time.

No sooner had I returned to my room than I got a call from Boxer. "I'm here," he said, "and there's another dude here with me, says he's waiting for you too."

When I went out to meet them, I found it was the other guy I had called. So I took the two of them over to meet the EOPS Director. He welcomed them, but was on his way to give an orientation to a group of students about to start the program.

"Come on to the meeting," the director said to my companions, "and when we finish, I'll fix you up with the paperwork to sign up for the program."

So I left them with Mr. Rangel, encouraging them to call me at home if they needed further help. I made the mistake of not taking their phone numbers, for I never heard from them again. I did not have Sharkey's number for reaching Boxer and the other guy's number, written on my hand, had long since washed away. All I know is that they must not have lasted very long because I never saw them on campus thereafter. I would have been glad to give them every bit of moral support at my disposal if only I had seen them again.

Just parenthetically, since I do not include Sharkey's full story later, I would like to note that Sharkey himself later attended City College for one year, then transferred to Palomar College in the northern part of San Diego County. There he studied computer assisted drafting and was about to get his certificate of completion as this book went to press in 1984. He was going to write for this book, but was too busy for now. Perhaps his fine story will appear in a later publication.

The first day of summer school I found Li'l Man just as he was getting out of class. He was with his brother Beto who had signed up for the same program. Li'l Man was wearing his finest *cholo* duds, all ironed and starched. His square-shouldered shirt had its long tails hanging out and his black shoes were so shiny that they demanded attention.

Beto obviously scorned his little brother's fascination with *cholismo*. They were a perfect study in contrasting philosophy in one family. Beto was dressed so that he fit right in with the rest of campus society, but Li'l Man seemed to delight in being an obvious standout.

Their personalities were just as different. Flamboyant Li'l Man greeted me waving a check. "Look what they gave us already," he shouted with glee, "a hundred fifty dollar check; now that's what I call easy money."

Beto stood by silently while Li'l Man bubbled over with the account of his first day of college.

"Of course we got too much homework already," Li'l Man complained. "That English teacher bitch expects us to look up fifty words in the dictionary by tomorrow."

"Why, that's good for you," I retorted. "Life is long and, who knows, someday you might want to write a book about your homeboys; so get all the education you can. I never expected to write a book, but I got educated. Then when I wanted to do it, I was able to."

"C'mon. Let's go cruising," said Li'l Man with a wave of his hand.

"What in?" I asked.

"I have a car," said Beto quietly.

"I'm goin' down to Broadway for lunch," I said. "I'll let you drop me there if you will."

When I saw his car, I almost flipped. It was a giant gold Cadillac—looked like a rich man's car even though it was an old model, about 1965. There was nothing super-fancy about it like the car club cars, but it was clean and in sparkling condition. They put me in the back seat of the convertible and when I sat down, I felt like I'd been swallowed up, the car was so big.

We were soon bopping down the street with stereo music blasting in our ears and the car bouncing up and down as the air whistled past our faces. The car even scraped the pavement sometimes from bouncing so low in back. It certainly was an exhilarating experience. Of course the music was too loud for any conversation until I got out, thanking them for the ride and hoping to see them tomorrow.

I never saw Li'l Man in college after that. In the coming weeks I ran into his brother a couple of times and asked, "How's it going?"

Beto assured me that he was doing fine. Then I would ask, "Is your brother around?"

"Oh, yeah, he's around somewhere."

"How's he doing in his classes?"

"Aw, I don't know," Beto replied. "He ain't none of my problem."

"You should be concerned with your brother," I pleaded, "try to encourage him."

"Naaa. I ain't my brother's keeper," drawled Beto in his easy-going manner. "Besides," and here he started getting a contemptuous gleam in his eye, "if he's gonna keep on with that *cholo* shit, I ain't gonna have nothing to do with him. Let him find his own transportation. You shoulda seen him today, Mr. McGuire."

"How so?"

"You know how the play 'Zoot Suit' has been showing up in LA?"

"Yes."

"Well, he and some other dudes drove all the way up there to see it. Now he's come back with a fancy *pachuco* outfit, baggy, pleated pants with big wide suspenders, a straw hat, and shades—the whole bit. He looks like *El Chuco* himself—and he wore it all to school today."

"I'll bet he looked neat," I said in defense of Li'l Man. "He always dresses spic and span."

"Neat enough, alright," Beto conceded, "but there's just no place for it—swaggering into class this morning like some banty rooster, swinging his watch on a gold chain as if he dropped out of the Forties."

"He'll grow out of it," I said soothingly. "He has you as his older brother to look up to."

"I can't even talk to him," Beto said woefully. "I try to talk some sense into him, but he just ignores me. And my father is even worse. They had a fight the other night and my father threw him out of the house."

"You mean he isn't living at home anymore?"

"Nope. Stays over at his girlfriend's place."

"Well, anyway," I concluded, "try to help him the best you can."

Beto just grunted disgustedly as we parted. "He'll never amount to anything."

The next thing I knew, Li'l Man had been shot. I was not teaching in the summer so I went out of town for two weeks. When I got back, the first thing I heard on the streets was that Li'l Man had been shot during the weekend.

"Is it bad?" I asked.

"Gonna be in the hospital several weeks."

"Damn," I spat, "four weeks gone in a five-week session and this happens."

I called his home and his sister told me his hospital phone number. When I called the hospital, there he was, and he told me the whole story.

"I was walkin' in the park last Sunday night with my friend Manny," he began.

"What park?" I interrupted.

55

"You know, man, Chicano Park; I wouldn't go walkin' at ten o'clock at night in no white boys' park."

"Sounds like it might have been safer somewhere else," I interjected with a little friendly banter.

"Yeah," he admitted dryly. "Anyhow, do you want to hear the story or not?"

"Sure."

"OK, then shut up and listen." Pause. "So here's how it went. We were just walkin' along minding our business when this carful of dudes pulls up. They shouted at us, 'Where you guys from?' Of course my homeboy Huero and I shouted, 'Logan Heights, *El Primero!*' So they yelled, 'We're from Sidro.' That's the gang down at San Ysidro, you know, Hilary."

"Yes, I know."

"So then one of those dudes pulls out a fuckin' big shotgun and yells at us, 'You'd better start running or we'll blast your ass right there.' So we lit out as fast as we could and I got hit anyway. Huero didn't get a thing."

"Where'd they hit you?"   •

"In the right arm and in the ribs; I've got a big hole in my arm."

"How long will you be in the hospital?"

"They say maybe two weeks, then a couple months in bed at home."

That phone conversation was on the night before I was scheduled to leave town again. I still had packing to do and could not get away to visit the hospital.

Next morning before my departure I phoned him again.

"I'm leaving town now," I said to Li'l Man, "but I would like to encourage you to make good use of your recuperation time. You have a fine mind so do some reading or writing."

"I can't write; they got my right arm."

"Oh, that's right. Sorry. Anyway, put your brain to work to try to figure some way that this won't happen to you or to others in the…"

"It sure won't happen to me again," he interrupted me, "because I'm going to be packing a piece myself from now on."

I groaned. "That's not what I meant; carrying a gun won't help anything. If one person shoots and another shoots back, there will be two people hurt instead of just one."

"Don't worry, Hilary, man," Li'l Man said with deliberate slowness, "I won't be the one who is hit."

"You can't be sure of that," I pointed out. "I'm no preacher, that's for sure, but the Bible says that those who live by the sword will die by the sword. And Jesus teaches us to forgive our enemies."

No comment from Li'l Man for a moment. Then he grimly changed the subject saying, "I have a private room here and there are security guards outside to be sure none of those dudes from Sidro come and stab me. They know I can testify against them. I can identify the car and some of the guys in it."

"That's good," I said, "You take care of yourself, now. And try to do some reading. See how those books are written; you might want to write your life story someday."

Li'l Man laughed as if he thought that would be impossible.

"Don't laugh," I chided. "Your life story would be a whole lot more interesting than most and you certainly have the capability to write it."

I had been saving my money for a trip to Switzerland and that is where I went after talking to Li'l Man. But my sympathies and hopes were still with him. So a few days later I wrote to him just to try to bring a new spark to his life while he lay in the hospital. Here is a copy of the letter.

Dear Li'l Man,

I was lying here on my bed in Friborg, Switzerland when I began thinking of you. Don't you know that you could be here instead of me? All it takes is about $400, an amount you could save in a short time.

Expand your horizons, Big Man; look up to what the world is offering you.

But what I am suggesting is not so much that you go to Switzerland, but that *you are a free human being*, able to put yourself into any place in the world. Why be in a hospital bed?

You are too *great* to die over a spot of ground in Logan Heights or anywhere else in the world. Your value is more than any spot of land. As the Bible says, "You are worth more than many sparrows."

The world is big—and beautiful—and you or any other young man you might shoot in retaliation are too young to die. You have something still to contribute to the world so that when you die as an old man, the world will be a better place because you passed through it.

You are intelligent; you can do it. You can climb up over the wall, the wall that holds you in. You can peek over the top of the wall and see the green grass, lush and moist, waiting for you. You can see the flowers and the mountains and the lakes and even the beautiful girls on the other side.

And because you are young and strong you can lift yourself over the wall and help your friends to climb over after you. Then you and your homeboys can hop down on the other side and spread your arms wide to the sunshine and breathe deep the sweet, fresh air and you will say, "Thank you, God, for giving me life today; thank you for all your gifts. I'm going to do something great and beautiful with it— something good for all the world—for all my homies."

That, my dear Big Man, is what I hope for you on this day and every day of the rest of your life.

Your very good friend,
Hilario

When I got back from my trip, I found Li'l Man on his feet again, quite well healed. He went back to finish his last year at high school (apparently he had lied about his age to get into the college summer program), but he got kicked out by the end of the first week. Thereafter I saw him on the streets a few times, dressed as a stone *cholo* and hanging out with the hard dudes who, from time to time, had been released from prison. Li'l Man asked me about getting into college for the fall, but it was too late; the semester had already started.

Next thing I knew, he was gone to Sacramento. His brother Beto was still in college and he told me that Li'l Man had been sent by his parents to stay with his grandmother in Sacramento and get into school up there.

Over the three years since then, Li'l Man has been dividing his life between Sacramento and San Diego. Many events have transpired in his life and he often calls me, sometimes comes to visit. He does not dress as a *cholo* anymore, says he has outgrown it. But he has never been back to college—yet.

But life is long, Li'l Man, and your potential is great. You may yet return to college or do whatever else your vigorous mind and personality desire. The world awaits you. Go for it!

Photo 8 - Li'l Man visits author in 1983—no more *cholo* dress
He died of an overdose circa 1986. The author and his wife
attended the funeral.

3 SHERMAN AND OTHER BARRIOS

Exactly a week and a day after the start of 1980 summer school, I got a call from a young man named Jorge. "Hey, man," he said, "I'm downstairs at the phone; why don't you come on down."

Going outside I met three new *cholos*. Jorge said that I had met him once before and told him about the EOPS program. Now he wanted in with his two friends from Sherman.

Sherman is a different barrio from the one whose members I had been dealing with heretofore. Of course I had nothing against that; in fact I was even glad. To have someone from Sherman come to me like this was evidence that they perceived me to be non-partisan, a neutral party, yet interested in the welfare of all. Sherman and Logan do not usually get along together, I had been told. A few times I had seen fights on the City College campus at noon when the students of San Diego High spilled over, scrambling for a quick cafeteria lunch at City. Whenever I sought out the source of the trouble from some of the teens from Logan, they would reply, "Aw, some dude from Sherman pushed one of our guys," or, "A couple of those *locos* from Sherman were hitting on our chicks."

Actually there are at least five different barrios represented at San Diego High. It was obvious to me that Logan had the largest contingent, followed by Sherman. Having never taken a census, something which I would not be inclined to do lest it stir up more rivalry in a matter in which I favor peace, inter-barrio relationships, I am not at all sure of the relative size of the numbers, but my strong feeling is that, after Sherman, Shelltown would be most heavily represented, followed closely by Lomas. Those are what I could call the four largest barrios in terms of numbers of students at SDHS.

Smaller numbers claim to be from Market Street and the 20s.

Each of the barrios has its own history and origin and I do not pretend to record that here. However, to give the reader a feel for the nature of barrio namings, let me say that I understand that Sherman is a neighborhood based around Sherman Junior High in the southern part of the Logan Heights area of the city of San Diego. Shelltown is directly east of Logan, the two being divided by Freeway 15. Lomas is named with the Spanish word for "hills" and is located to the north of Logan in the part of San Diego called Golden Hill, just east of and overlooking downtown San Diego where Market Street barrio has its roots. The 20s are found in the area of 20th Street near Market.

All of these neighborhoods tend to send students to San Diego High. This natural flow is of course disrupted by busing which scatters the barrios, though not to a great extent.

Anyway, the different barrios at SDHS generally get along pretty well together. In fact, compared to such mixtures of gang neighborhoods at schools in Los Angeles, the San Diego youth are extremely peaceful.

Having been familiar with the Los Angeles scene as well as that in San Diego, I believe that this relative serenity is due to not only the less violent nature of the San Diego youth, but also to the more repressive character of the San Diego police force. SDHS is especially well covered by the SDPD since the school is right downtown where the police are most concentrated. Thus, whenever a group of as small as about twenty-five youths begins to congregate, there are suddenly half a dozen police cars on the spot.

Still, at different times it takes the police ten or fifteen minutes to respond and in that time I have seen groups of up to two hundred *cholos* and *cholas* gather to watch fights between two on up to half-a-dozen *vatos*.

Gang fighting in the sense of hordes of fifteen or twenty dudes flailing at another group with chains and knives, I have never seen in my dozen years of involvement. That sort of fight seems to be a thing of the past, made obsolete by the ready availability of guns.

Nowadays there are mainly two types of altercations: either a small group involved in fisticuffs or drive-by shootings. The latter, very common in Los Angeles to this day, are much more rare in San Diego, although the incidence in recent years has been sufficient to cause much furor in the press and for the police. Thus did the gang detail of the SDPD have its origin relatively recently, in 1978.

Getting back to Jorge and his homies from Sherman, I had to tell them, "Gosh, guys, it's too late now to get into the summer program, but I'll take you over to the college and show you where to register for the fall."

They were game for that so I gave them a brief tour of the enrollment area and the financial aid office. That was all it took.

Come fall, there was Jorge, quietly going to math and English classes as he pursued a degree in refrigeration and air conditioning technology.

I happened to see him in my spare-time job working for the EOPS tutoring program when I was not teaching classes. Jorge came in with his math book for a little assistance. The name of his barrio was represented by a tattoo on his arm, "SM."

He did not need much help with his math; he understood it perfectly, just wanted help to review for an occasional test.

As I saw this quiet, handsome youth through the weeks of the semester, I learned that he was getting an A in his math class and was doing well in his other classes.

"I sure am proud of you, Jorge," I said, "and I'll bet you're proud of yourself, too."

"Sure am," he replied, "but it doesn't come easy; I go home at night and I study hard."

"I'm sure you do," I replied, "but you know, Jorge, that nothing worthwhile in life comes easily. We've got to struggle to help ourselves as well as others."

"Yeah," he affirmed with a shrug of his big shoulders, his dark eyes full of his serious efforts to get an education.

Photo 9 - Jorge from Sherman showing hand sign "S"

"Are any of your homies from Sherman here this fall?" I asked.

"Naw, they didn't want to come."

"Well," I said, "when they see how well you're doing, maybe it'll encourage them to come next spring."

"Maybe," he said with a wistful sound of hope.

Since then I have seen Jorge on campus for several semesters. It takes at least four semesters (two years) to get through a degree program at a community college.

Today in 1983 I was walking through the college cafeteria. I heard a gentle calling of my name. I turned and there was Jorge, sitting at a table flanked by several girls.

"Jorge," I said, "how the heck are you doing?"

"Fine," he replied, "I graduated last spring with a degree in machine shop technology."

"Great. So what are you doing around here?"

"I'm taking a few more classes and I'm the treasurer for the Student Body Association, the ASB."

"Wow," I said, "that's really terrific." I noted he was sporting a New Wave hair style and that he had apparently changed his major.

I told him about this book, *Homeboys in College* and he suggested he might be willing to be in it.

"Sure," he said, "you can interview me; I don't have time to write anything. Call me at my office in the ASB sometime."

When I contacted him, he told me much of his life story. He was born in San Luis, Mexico and lived there for five years before his family came to the United States. He spent most of his youth in the Sherman barrio, then went to Roosevelt Junior High where he met Shady (pictured on back cover).

"I'm going to write a book myself," Jorge said, "about Shady's life and mine."

"Good idea," I told him, "I've always said that if the homeboys would write their own stories, they'd be more interesting than anything I can write about them."

"Yeah, so don't steal my idea," Jorge cautioned. "We've been friends for a long time, Hilario, and I respect you, but don't you steal my idea or I'll never speak to you again."

"Well," I revealed, "I've already taken Shady's picture for my book. He has a terrific mind and is taking computers."

"That's OK, man, but the whole story will be in my book; I'm gonna call it *How Shady Went to College.*"

"That'll be great," I said, "but anyway, tell me more about yourself. How old are you?"

"Twenty-one. I've had my ups and downs in life, but I'm at the peak right now. I studied one year of machine shop in high school and two years in college. I have an Associate degree now, but I'm not going to stop there; I'm going to D-Q University in Davis and then on to Harvard Law School, the finest law school in the country. And I'm going to be a lawyer.

"From Cyclone 13 (that was my nickname in the Sherman barrio), I have become a machinist, metal worker, artist, musician, and actor. And now I'm going to study to be a lawyer."

"That's great," I said. "Power to you, brother, but you know that it's not going to come easy; nothing comes easy anymore when you're an adult."

"I know, Hilary, man, I know, but I can do it."

"I know you can, Jorge. Now tell me what kind of musician you are."

"I play the saxophone already and I'm studying piano right now here at City College."

"What kind of art do you do and where did you get your nickname?"

"I do all kinds of art—have been drawing since I was in second grade, mostly pencil sketches and pen and ink. Now that I'm a machinist, I have the ability of working with metal.

"And you know, Hilary," Jorge continued with a more animated voice, "you know where I got my nickname?"

"No."

"The thirteen I got from my birthday; I was born on Friday the 13th—a real lucky day that was. But I got all crazy mad at the world one time and my homeboys called me Cyco."

"How do you spell that?" I asked.

"C-y-c-o."

"Does that mean the same as P-s-y-c-h-o?"

"Yes, but this is in Spanish. So, anyway, from Cyco I developed it to Cyclone 13."

"I know that the number thirteen appears in wall graffiti frequently as referring to marijuana since 'm' is the thirteenth letter of the alphabet," I interjected.

"Sure, Hilario, and we smoke a little weed and drink a little booze too, just like the white boys. I'll have you over to toke a 'j' with me sometime, but that's not what the thirteen in my name means."

"And, oh, there's one thing more about my barrio, Hilary; be sure to put this in your book. I have a son and I named him after my neighborhood. His name is the same as mine, but with Sherman as his middle name. I'll be sure that Jorge Sherman is proud of his heritage."

"That name has a good solid ring to it, solid and handsome, just like you, Jorge."

"You bet, Hilary, and there are two more things I want you to mention in your book—MEChA and D-Q University."

"I know all about MEChA," I said, "the campus organization to encourage college education among Chicano youth, but where is D-Q and what does it stand for?"

"It's in Davis and it means Deganawidah-Quetzalcoatl. Its purpose is to foster study in Chicano and American Indian cultures."

When he spelled that name for me, I was able to do further research on it. I learned that it was founded in 1977 and is a fully accredited liberal arts junior college offering Associate of Arts and Associate of Science degrees just like most community colleges do. But D-Q is a small private school with a mere 122 students in the year my source recorded. Having myself come from a small, private JC, I recognize that there are many advantages to such a school such as more personal attention from instructors and a less distracted atmosphere for academic pursuits.

So Jorge has a goal to become a lawyer. That may require a few more years, but he will still have a long life ahead of him and the ability to help the world in many different ways.

Whatever happens in Jorge's life, he has the kind of quiet determination and devotion to duty which it takes for success in any field. He is an example to all who see and hear about him.

But each one of us has a different style, dear reader, so whatever yours is, make the most of your own particular talents. Only you can do the things you can do the way you can do them. *Si se puede*; yes you can—and you must—not only for yourself, but for the ones you love.

4 *LA NUEVA FRONTERA NEUTRAL*

In my math classes I am noted for being a teacher who sticks to the subject and constantly drives on into the material of the course. But each semester, after I am well familiar with the students, I spend about fifteen minutes letting them know something about my out-of-class interests.

Thus it was that one of my students, Jack Sparks, came up to me at the end of a class in November 1980 and said, "I'd like to read your book *Hopie and the Los Homes Gang.*"

Several days later Sparks came to me saying, "I liked your book and I have some ideas to help your work with the *cholos.*"

Through the years, of course, I have heard that line dozens of times and it usually comes to nothing whatsoever. Coming from this bespectacled, fifty-two-year-old man who constantly came to class, even in winter, wearing the same pair of cut-off shorts and sneakers, I took this statement very much with a grain of salt.

We sat down, however, in the cafeteria and started chatting. This fellow had always been outstanding in my class for having some previous knowledge about any topic I might discuss, even the history of mathematicians like Euler and Paschal. Though I like to encourage students to make comments, this know-it-all attitude got to be rather tiresome both to me and to the members of the class.

It was, therefore, not surprising that Sparks insisted, "I know all about *cholos*."

"Oh, yeah?" I said with skepticism in my voice.

"Sure. I've been a street person all my life and I was raised with Chicanos back in Arizona."

"So what ideas do you have to help my homeboys?" I asked. "What they need most are jobs and education so they can get better jobs."

"We can start a contracting business for small jobs like yard work and clean-up around construction sites," he said.

I scoffed at that. "Sure enough," I snorted, "but how are we going to do that without money for mowers and shovels and a truck?"

Undaunted, Sparks droned on. "Or we could start out cheap in the costume jewelry business."

"Who knows anything about that?" I asked.

"I do; during my many-faceted career I have at one time or another made my living in that business."

I could tell by the looks of him that it had not been a lucrative enterprise, but I was eager for any way I could find to give jobs to my homies who wandered the streets aimlessly while college and high school classes were going on. Invariably my conversations with out-of-school homeboys indicated they would prefer jobs rather than going back to school.

"So how do we start," I asked, "and how much money does it take?"

"Oh, about a hundred fifty bucks," Sparks said casually.

"A hundred fifty bucks!" I shouted. "Why so much?"

"Well, you need at least three pairs of needle-nose pliers and those don't come cheap. Then we need beads and feathers and chains and charms and..."

"Hold it; hold it right there. There must be some less expensive way to get started."

Always ready with a new idea, Sparks said, "Well, yes there is. With Christmas coming on and lots of parties being planned, you could go into the mistletoe business."

"Oh yeah?"

"Sure. People will pay fifty cents for a sprig, so all you need to do is go find some mistletoe and start cleaning up."

I was not so easily convinced that it would work, but the idea of taking homeboys out to get in touch with nature had always appealed to me since my first involvement back in East LA. I believe in the therapeutic value of contact with nature over a long period of time and that there is no time like the present to begin.

So I planned a mistletoe hunt, familiar as I was with its growth pattern from my early life back in Oklahoma where mistletoe is the state flower.

On Saturday morning I picked up Chango and a friend named Joker at their homes in Logan Heights. Chango had been out of school all semester and had not yet found a job so the prospect of making some money was very appealing to him.

Though I had phoned Chango on Friday and he had said he would be ready and would tell Joker, yet when I arrived at 9:15 Saturday morning, Chango was sound asleep. I had an extensive chat with his father using my broken Spanish while waiting for Chango to get ready.

At Joker's house we had to go through the same process before we finally headed for the hills.

Unlike LA, the wide open spaces and mountain foothills are within easy reach, little more than five miles from any of the San Diego barrios. So we were soon cruising along in the countryside.

"Keep an eye open for oak trees," I said, "the mistletoe will be growing in those."

"What's mistletoe?" they asked.

"Haven't you ever seen that stuff they use at Christmas parties? They hang it up and when a girl walks under it, all the guys can kiss her."

"Oh, yeah," said Chango, "but what are we doing?"

"Well, the stuff grows on trees in big clumps and we're going to try to find some and take it back to sell it."

"Does that mean we have to climb trees?"

"Sure, don't all young people climb trees?"

"I don't. I don't," came from both of them.

"Don't worry, I'll do the climbing," I assured them.

But finding the right trees was not easy. We drove for miles and miles, eyeing every tree in sight, but with no luck. I could not understand whether there was just no mistletoe in this area or that someone had beat us to it.

Finally, however, we did spot some trees growing in a tiny creek bed. There seemed to be clumps of thick green leaves in various places.

"Let's go for it," I shouted as I bounded from the car.

But to my amazement my friends seemed reluctant.

"Aren't there snakes in that grass?" Chango asked.

"Naw. If there were, they'd be more afraid of you than you are of them. Just don't step on one and you'll be OK. Trust me; I've been hiking all my life."

So the guys were with me until we hit a barbed wire fence. They had absolutely no idea how to get through it. I found a spot halfway between two posts and put my foot on the second wire from the bottom.

"Come on, guys," I said as I lifted the top wire with my hands. "You can crawl through here now. Just bend down and slide through, but be careful not to raise up too soon or those barbs will tear your shirt."

Thus Chango and Joker encountered and conquered their first barbed wire fence. Once they were free in the wild country, they soon warmed to the situation. They found a creek and pranced back and forth jumping over it. They picked up rocks and threw at birds.

"We're tripping out," I heard Joker tell Chango as they picked up sticks for pounding the brush and started poking their noses into hollow trees.

After I had pointed out lichen growing on the north side of a tree, they asked me about another growth they found.

"What's that, Hilario?" Chango cried out as he pointed at a grayish protuberance jutting out from the trunk of a tree.

"That's shelf fungus," I said. "See how it forms a sort of little knick-knack shelf on the trunk of the tree?"

Chango and Joker grunted acknowledgement, then sprinted on ahead of me, jumping back and forth across the stream, talking to each other in Spanish as they intently examined *ranas* (frogs) in the creek and *huesos* (bones) of an old dead cow.

They cavorted around the bones having a great time picking them apart and joking with each other using expressions like *pinche mensote* (stupid dummy).

One of the bones, part of a cow's facial structure, they took with them to bring home and make a mask of some sort.

I was still looking for mistletoe even though the youngsters had little understanding of my purpose. I was about to give up when I sighted a broken-down but still-living willow tree. It seemed to have an exceptionally thick growth in some places so I went closer to see. Sure enough, the tree had many clumps of mistletoe, so hidden by the tree's own leaves that the mistletoe was almost indistinguishable.

"Come on, guys," I shouted with elation. "I found some."

They did not seem impressed when they finally saw what I was after, but Chango readily allowed Joker and me to boost him up into the tree to test his kinship with his namesake, the monkey.

A gigantic batch of mistletoe, about five feet wide from one side to another, was situated on a one-inch thick branch.

"Break the branch," I shouted to Chango. "We want to keep it all together if we can."

"It won't break," he replied.

"So put your whole weight on it," I suggested. "Hang on it."

It worked like a charm and down came mistletoe, Chango and all.

Joker and I caught all falling objects and we all roared with laughter. We danced around our prize as if it were a slain game animal.

Joker then set off to show his prowess. He climbed far up to a height whose accessibility even I had doubted. Soon he was tossing down more giant branches of mistletoe.

Chango was also finding more at lower levels. Within one-half hour we had so much that I began to doubt we could get it all into the car. So I called a halt to the pillaging even though the gathering of mistletoe is no damage to the ecology. In fact, since mistletoe is a parasite which sucks the life from trees, it is actually a benefit to the trees to remove it. But I wanted to leave some growing freshly in case we should care to come back for more some other day.

As we gathered our spoils for the trip to the car, I gave them both a triumphant hand-clap and shouted, "Good work, big team; I'm giving each of you ten dollars for today's work and if we sell the stuff, you'll get a share of the proceeds."

So we tripped on home and I gave them a crisp twenty dollar bill to be split between them.

Sad to say, even though we kept the mistletoe in water, it all died before the Christmas season arrived. And Sparks never thought of a good place to sell it, even if we went back for more. Our marketing skills were not as great as our collection ability.

Anyway, it was fun and my homies had a great experience while making some money.

My student Jack Sparks, the fifty-two-year-old, jack-of-all-trades and master-of-none, had an apartment which was perfect for students to work in making costume jewelry. So I bank-rolled him with $160 to purchase materials necessary for the business. We thought of calling our enterprise "Neutral Ground" because we hoped to have homeboys from all different barrios working for us. One day, however, after Sparks had consulted with several *cholos* in the college cafeteria, high school students eating their lunch there, we decided on an even better name: *La Nueva Frontera Neutral*, meaning The New Neutral Frontier.

Here is how we started our business.

I saw two *vatos* standing on the street waiting for the high school to let out. One was wearing a tank top with a bandana around his head. He looked like a hard dude if ever there was one. The other dude with him seemed too drunk or doped up to do anything, but I walked right up to them and said, "Would you guys like to have a job?"

"Sure, man," said the sober one while the other fellow nodded his head groggily. "Just let me see if I can pick up on one of these chicks first. If I don't score, we'll work for you."

So I sat there with them on the giant San Diego City College sign literally watching all the girls go by.

When the crowd had passed, the sober one said, "OK, man, how much do you pay, man?"

"Three dollars an hour," I informed him, "the current minimum wage."

"That sounds good to me," blurted the other dude, his head wobbling with lack of self-control.

Both of them were soon working under the guidance of Sparks at his apartment. He showed them how to select matching stones for an earring set, then glue on tiny caps which would fit onto the ear. They also made necklaces with different silvery and gold or semi-precious stone pendants.

When I came back a few hours later, I was quite impressed with the beautiful results and paid the guys for their time.

"Now all we have to do is sell them," I noted light-heartedly. "Do you guys think you could sell these to any of your friends?"

"Naw, man," came from the homeboys in unison, "but we'll be glad to work tomorrow if you want us."

"Sure," said Sparks. "Come at 3 and bring a couple of other guys if you want."

"What about my girlfriend?" asked one of them.

"That would be fine," I assured him.

When the homeboys left, Sparks said, "They both did fine, but especially the sober one."

"Can you sell some of this stuff?" I asked.

"Sure. I have lots of contacts on the street."

As the weeks went by, Sparks did manage to sell our products, at least enough to keep us supplied with beads and feathers for more assembling. Feather jewelry such as earrings and hatbands were very "in" at that time as part of the western style craze. Especially popular were what Sparks called "dangles," double and triple rawhide strips with fluffy feathers and wooden beads on them, all of which could be clipped onto hat brims or lapels or the rear view mirrors of cars by means of an electrician's alligator clip. Within a year, however, those alligator clips were outlawed in San Diego because they were also being used as "roach clips" to hold the butt of a marijuana cigarette as it burned down too low for cool handling.

It was never hard to find workers to fit into our program. We decided that the purpose of *La Nueva Frontera Neutral* would be to help *cholos*, the harder, the better, get jobs or education or both.

I was the recruiter and Sparks was the teacher for the costume jewelry branch of the operation. I would approach hard dudes even if I did not know them (in fact I preferred to use this job as a means to meet new people) and invite them to do a couple or three hours of work. The prospect of immediate cash spending money, which I made part of our policy because I believed that such prompt payoff would be very encouraging to them, always appealed to them. Also the lack of postponed paydays promoted a sense of trust which I saw as the first step in establishing a link between the *cholo* population and the "straight" world of work and school.

Sparks did such an outstanding job of relating to whomever I brought to him that I soon thought of him as my partner. We adopted the motto: "Shake the hand of a *cholo* today," because it indicated the initial break-through necessary to work with these youths who to most of society appear to be very alienated and forbidding as they stand defiantly on street corners, often blocking much of the walkway.

So I would make the initial contact and Sparks would make the secondary one, take them into his apartment and start teaching them how to make hatbands, dangles, or whatever.

One of my long-time beliefs is that "youth and beauty are gifts of nature, but old age is a work of art." That means that we are given by nature and the Creator whatever beauty we have when we are young, but then we build our old age using those gifts. Since what we become in our old age is a result of our human efforts, our old age is a work of art.

Sparks, at age fifty-two, seemed to have taken all the gifts of nature and all the experiences of his life and molded them into a magnificent work of art. He was a fellow who could feel comfortable with anyone, could accept all persons with respect, and had the ability to pass on some of his wisdom and knowledge of life. He was a great asset on The New Neutral Frontier. He never asked the *cholos* what neighborhood they were from or what status they might have with the law. The *vatos* knew they were on neutral ground where only the future and the present would be considered.

Sometimes we had six or seven guys crowded into that studio apartment. Since only three could fit at the table, the others did their work on the bed or floor. It was all a great pleasure to me to see such a diverse crew from different barrios all getting along together and working industriously.

Never once did we have a fight or any disturbance other than the normal bustle involved with the work and the comings and goings of so many people.

The landlady was quite alarmed at first, but when I explained our purposes, she agreed to let us continue as long as we caused no disruption to the lives of the other tenants.

Sparks handled the young fellows so well that he never had to be a disciplinarian, though I am sure that part of his ability with the young people was that he was able to create an atmosphere in which all knew clearly what was to be done and that no untoward behavior would be tolerated. Instead of a disciplinarian, therefore, Sparks was a teacher, counselor, and friend.

Sparks had been in two branches of the service, had worked at innumerable jobs including small appliance repair and the manufacture of costume jewelry. "Most recently," he told me, "I have been making my livelihood by gambling, but I just got sick of it and decided I want to do something more significant with my life. I have always liked things of the mind, especially the occult and parapsychology, so I decided to go back to college and major in psychology."

He had taken a few courses in some junior college back in Arizona and now at the age of fifty-two he just dropped everything and was going to finish college. Thus he was a perfect role model for our clients, a clear demonstration that anyone can start a new life at any age.

And Sparks was a street person. He had been hanging out in the downtown area, sharing an apartment with a gambling buddy for twenty dollars a week when he first started back to college.

A greater partner I could not imagine for *La Nueva Frontera Neutral*. At least that is what I thought for a few months. But the troubles I had with Sparks, which eventually led to our disassociation 1 ½ years later shall not be part of this story. Suffice it to say that without him I would never have accomplished the establishment of this organization to give jobs and education to *cholos*.

For that I am eternally grateful to him. Our partnership may resume someday.

The homeboys were quite willing to make costume jewelry in the privacy of Sparks' room, but never could we devise a gimmick to induce them to be publicly associated with the product.

Joker was standing in the front of McDonald's one day when I came along with a cardboard covered with the neck chains that he had helped fashion.

"School will be out in a few minutes," I said referring to the dismissal hour of the high school.

"Yeah," he said amiably, "I'm waiting for a friend of mine."

"If you'll sell some of these things to your friends, you can keep fifty cents for each sale you make," I suggested.

"Naw, man," he said with no explanation. He was friendly, but firm with his refusal.

So I just stood there beside him as the students started piling out of the high school. As the first *cholas* came by, I held out the card with its shiny contents and said, "Anyone want to buy a necklace; Joker and I made 'em."

The girls just walked on by as Joker turned to me with a scowl and said, "Hey, what you doin', man?"

"Just trying to sell the stuff," I explained. "You know, if I'm gonna keep paying you guys to work, we've got to sell the stuff to keep going."

"Uh huh, but not beside me," and he walked away.

We had the same experience when we finally got permission to set up a table to sell our jewelry on the college campus. No matter how much commission we offered, none of our homies would sit at that table. So Sparks became our ace salesman. He bought himself a cowboy hat on which to display our hand-made hat bands and from which to dangle one of our fancy feather dangles. There he sat behind the table for hours on end as the campus representative of the college-recognized club, *La Nueva Frontera Neutral.*

I wish I could say that our business was a huge success, but it was not. I kept putting out more and more money to support Sparks' schemes and to pay the homies. For one guy to work three hours cost me $10 at $3.35 per hour so one can imagine that expenses mounted rapidly when an average of three homies per day were working that long on five days each week. Besides that, Sparks would come to me saying, "I saw some really pretty Austrian crystal crosses and dew-drops which would make fantastic pendants and earrings."

So I would shell out more and more money, but with little coming in. We could not go on that way for long.

Of course Jack Sparks had yet another idea. "Why not incorporate? As a non-profit corporation we could solicit donations from various companies."

"Sure," I said scornfully, "and who's gonna do the soliciting? I'm sure not cut out for that kind of begging."

"I'll do it," he promised.

We bought a book which tells how to incorporate without a lawyer and Sparks typed up something like fifty pages of paperwork. We sent it to the Secretary of State in Sacramento. Several months later we received notice that *La Nueva Frontera Neutral* had been approved as a non-profit corporation in the State of California.

So with the blessing of the State of California we continued our process of encouraging the homies with jobs and information about financial aid for college. If they were not of college age yet, we encouraged them to stick it out in high school.

Sparks managed to make contacts with a couple of relatively large distributors of feather and bead jewelry. We thus got orders for $150 and $200 worth of our products at wholesale prices. So we had deadlines to meet and several days' work for half-a-dozen homeboys. They were so pleasant and cooperative that it was hard to believe that some of them, as indicated by little teardrop tattoos in the corners of their eyes, had spent several months or years of their lives in jail and that all of them had long histories of trouble with school authorities and police. It just confirmed my belief that people respond according to how they are treated and that if you treat people with respect and kindness, most of them will react positively.

Unfortunately our business deals were not as favorable as our personal relations. Sparks always seemed to offer our wares for sale, whether wholesale or retail, at prices lower than our cost. Thus I was constantly losing money. Even non-profit corporations need to make enough money to stay afloat.

I had always had a policy of never spending more money than I had on hand, but having Sparks for a partner changed all that. He purchased leather and feathers, etc. from different companies and managed to do it on credit—my credit—without my knowledge. I blew up.

My ranting had no more effect on Sparks than water on a duck's back. He kept spending more money than we could possibly make.

"What about your idea to solicit donations from various companies?" I asked.

Nothing ever came of it.

About that time I was invited to be on the Planning Advisory Council (commonly known as the PAC Board) of San Diego County's CETA Organization. The Comprehensive Employment and Training Act (CETA) is Federal legislation to train and employ needy persons. The Board acted until the end of 1982 as one of two federally-mandated sources of citizen input.

There were about twenty persons on PAC and I was selected because of my long-time interest in the employment and education of homeboys. The fact that I had published a book and had established a non-profit corporation was some indication to the selection committee that I would be able to cope with the bureaucracy and paperwork involved in PAC Board activity.

I must admit, however, that in the nearly two full years I served on that Board, I often thought my time would have been better spent out on the streets helping young people more directly.

There was one accomplishment, however, which directly related to the homeboys during that time. It was a project espoused by Mayor Pete Wilson who has since become one of California's two United States Senators in Washington.

Starting in about the fall of 1980, the San Diego newspapers had started publicizing the local gang problem. The police department claimed that it had not been very public with the problem in the past lest publicity make the gang members more active. Mayor Wilson took action when his Crime Commission indicated in a report that the number of identifiable gangs had risen from five to thirty-eight in the past five years.

Through a convoluted chain of events involving the establishment of a Street Youth Task Force under Deputy Chief of Police Ken O'Brien, the idea of a San Diego Street Youth Project came up for CETA funding. My only input as a member of the PAC Board was to beg that a sizeable portion of the funds would go for salaries for the youths themselves. As finally approved, though, the funding went for hiring six counselors, an executive director, and paying the rental expenses for offices in San Ysidro and Logan Heights.

The emphasis of the counselors was to guide the young people into various educational and employment opportunities which are available in the community. I mention this because later in this story, the Street Youth Program will be seen as a contributing factor in leading some of the homeboys to college.

About the same time as all of this high-level governmental concern with the homeboys, I had made a very low-level proposal of my own, a small project that Sparks and I could handle through our infant organization, *La Nueva Frontera Neutral.*

Since it has always seemed to me that proficiency in reading and writing the English language is essential to progress in American society and that many of my homeboys had a great deficiency in this regard, I conceived a Homeboy Writing Project.

A reading project was out of the question because reading is such a passive operation. I wanted the homies to be reinforced by seeing physical evidence of their work right in front of them. Writing is such an active operation that it would improve their reading and spelling capabilities while giving them the experience of learning to communicate on paper.

The Writing Project would pay the youngsters by the hour so that there would be no penalty for those who were having trouble getting started or who would need to seek constant spelling aid either from the instructor or the dictionary. I visualized Sparks and myself as the instructors, each supervising about five writers.

And what would the homeboys write? Just any kind of writing, anything which would come to mind, would help improve skills, but if specific direction was needed, I had some suggestions ready. Psychologists have long recognized that writing one's experiences is a helpful process. It helps show people clearly where they have been. Once that is seen, it is easier to take a deliberate step into the future, to plan a strategy of life. Also, if something is bothering the writer, putting it down on paper helps to get it off one's chest and to make clear just what the problem is. Thus writing is seen as an expurgation, a cleansing of the psyche. One feels better when troubles are all out on paper.

To be more specific, I suggested that the Writing Project concentrate on each writer's relationships with parents, teachers, classmates, fellow homeboys, rival gang members, and police. These relationships could be explored by first recording mere experiences, then analyzing those, telling feelings of that particular moment, feelings now, and what relationship the writer would like to foster in the future.

I wrote the proposal and submitted it to Mayor Wilson's secretary thinking that this project could be implemented very inexpensively as an adjunct to whatever other project the city might fund. As one expert example of a professional program recommending the kind of writing I was suggesting, I referred to Dr. Ira Progoff's Intensive Journal Process, about which more can be found in any extensive library. I also suggested that a compilation of such writing might help politicians, police, teachers, parents, and any interested person to understand better the thoughts and experiences of the homeboys.

Never did I hear a word from the Mayor's Office, but some of the ideas formulated at that time are the background for my inclusion of personal writings of the homeboys and homegirls in the latter portions of this book. Those writings do not totally fit my idea of the Writing Project, but they are a start. I still hope to someday implement or see implemented the kind of self-helping Homeboy Writing Project which is described above.

My association with Jack Sparks dragged on for another year with the ideas of our organization spreading a bit, even without money. All the homeboys we came in contact with knew that we were keeping our ears open for jobs. When we had no job to offer or to refer them to, at least we would point to the schools and colleges as means of self-improvement. Though they complained that they needed a job right now, we would point out, "Life is long and a few years spent on education now will bear tremendous fruits later."

But *La Nueva Frontera Neutral* had less and less money and jobs for the young people so we slowly slackened our activity. Finally Sparks and I parted company and my only contacts with the homeboys became those I had on campus or on the streets nearby.

5 AUTOBIOGRAPHY OF A   ·
COLLEGIATE HOMEBOY

In the spring of 1983 I had a student named Martha in one of my mathematics classes. One day, after I had revealed to the class the existence of my corporation designed to help homeboys get education and jobs, she introduced me to her boyfriend Luis who had recently moved from Los Angeles to San Diego.

Martha had encouraged him to enroll in City College and he was doing really well. When I told him my idea of writing a book in which homeboys in college would tell their life stories and how they happened to arrive at this point in their lives, he liked the idea.

As mentioned earlier, I had been for a long time suggesting to my homeboy friends that they should do the writing, that I would just be the editor. My thought was that they would write something of more interest to their fellow homeboys than most of what I might write.

When you read the following story, I think you will agree that this young man has come through a great many difficulties and that he is very much to be admired in his continuing efforts to improve his life with education and legitimate employment.

Here is his autobiography.

"My name is Luis Fernando Garcia. I was born in Mexicali, Mexico. When I was two, my dad died and left me and my mom alone. When I was three, we moved to East LA. My mom, two aunts, several cousins, and I lived in the projects called Ramona Gardens. The name of this barrio is Big Hazard. It is very big; it has seven *klickas* or gang cliques: The Diablos for *veteranos* in their thirties, Termites, Peewees, *Chicos*, *Sietes* for *vatos* twenty to twenty-two years of age, Jokers for ages seventeen to nineteen, and Nite Owls for twelve to fifteen-year-olds. There are a lot of factories to the south of our neighborhood. The San Bernardino Freeway is to the west; to the north are General Hospital and Hazard Park.

"I went to Evergreen Elementary School. Everything was pretty cool the first years there. It wasn't until the fifth grade that I started getting into trouble, fighting and ditching. That was also the first time that I smoked weed. I liked it. There we were, Wolf and I and Reuben, three little punks all high on weed. What a sight we were in Wabash Park ditching school. Wolf said he had stolen it from his big brother Rock (and I do mean solid as a rock).

"That was a big day for me because the three of us and nine other young hoodlums started a little club called The Artistics. But there was nothing artistic about us; all we knew how to do was write on the walls. We all got jumped in (the initiation process). Somebody counted forty seconds while three others beat the hell out of us—or tried to.

"We were all trouble-makers. There was another club called Lil Block. They had at least twenty-two members, but we had them running around like chickens without heads.

"It wasn't until the sixth grade that we all started getting into sniffing glue and paint. One night things got out of hand. For the first time we needed help. The boys from Lil Block got some back-up from a neighborhood called Gerathy Loma and hit us up. The *vatos* from Lil Block tricked us; they made us run after them and we all ran into their trap. The guys from GL came out and put a boot to our butts. They stabbed Midget four times, once in the stomach, three times in the back. Now we were the ones running around like headless chickens. We called the police. When we heard the sirens real close, we got out of Dodge fast.

"Midget was in Children's Hospital for 3 ½ weeks. We all visited him and there we decided to break up. We were smaller, younger, and only twelve of us; we knew we couldn't hang with those dudes from Gerathy Loma. So the Artistics were no more. Everybody went his separate way. We never saw each other again.

"In the summer I got into Big Hazard 7's (*Sietes*). I was about fourteen years old, yet was considered big enough and tough enough for this older group.

"In the seventh grade I went to Hollenbeck Junior High. There I was suspended five times for fighting and was arrested at school once for gang activities.

"For the eighth grade my mom made me go to school in Huntington Park, Nimitz Junior High. I did pretty well there all during the eighth and ninth grades because I was alone. None of my homeboys went there. I had only one fight in Nimitz and that was with a Cuban. He spit on my hushpuppies when I was walking by him. So I kicked his ass good and took his shoes and put them in the toilet.

"I went to Roosevelt High for the tenth grade. I was trying to keep out of trouble and I did for about three months. Then things started getting out of hand. My neighborhood and another one called Third Street were going at it hard for about a month. One day five of my homies and I were standing around ditching and smoking a joint when we spotted these four smacks, you know, sissies, *chavalas*. They were walking real fast. We knew they were from Third Street so we took off after them yelling at them and calling them girls. Three of us ran across the grass after them while the other three ran down the hallway to the doors that lead to the street. We had them in the middle; they had no place to run. We surprised them—I could see it in their faces. But they still hung tough and took the beating.

"I happened to look over my shoulder and saw a black and white zooming toward us. I yelled *placa* (cops)! We all ran in different directions. I ran straight to a vacant house nearby. We all got away, but the narcs at school had seen five of our faces. I was one of them. The next day I was in my history class. A narc came to the room and took me, Smokey, off to the office. There I found my friends Fox, Sonny, Blackie, and Puppet. They searched us and told us a bunch of crap trying to scare us. All we did was laugh. This made them very angry so they expelled us from the whole LA City School District.

Photo 10 - Luis Garcia from LA's Big Hazard barrio

"My mom was pissed off. She made me go to Bell Garden High by bus every day. That's in the Montebello School District. I finished the tenth grade there and half a semester in the eleventh. I was getting tired of waking up at 5:00 a.m. so I ran away. I lived with my homeboy Fabian in his aunt's garage for 2 ½ months. We sold drugs to eat and buy clothes. Mostly we sold weed and angel dust.

"One night we got busted and we were sent to Juvie (Juvenile Hall) at Los Padrinos.

"When I got out, I felt real good to be free, but not for long. My stepfather was giving me a hard time. I couldn't take it. One night I came home all kooled out with a gun in my hand and almost shot him in the head. Somehow I snapped out of it and I knew I had to get away.

"So I moved to San Diego to live with my Aunt Rosa and Cousin Jesse. I tried to go back to school, but couldn't hack it. The place was Mission Bay High School. I went for about two months and dropped out.

"I went to work at a restaurant, but I really didn't like the job so I quit. I didn't know what I was going to do. I liked San Diego a lot more than LA, no smog, beaches real close, and a lot more peaceful. I could actually sleep well at night, no sounds of guns or fighting in the street. I liked the sleeping best of all.

"But I didn't know what to do. So I joined the Army, saw Germany, Panama, and many states in the US.

"Came back after a couple of years and felt lost and lonely for about 1 ½ months until I met Martha and my whole life did a three-sixty.

"Martha started cleaning out my life, making me do things I really didn't want to do, but I did them just to please her. She was the one who made me stand in line and fill out papers to go to City College. We had a couple of little fights, Martha and I did, but she won.

"She made me realize I needed to go back to school to better myself, to re-learn things I had forgotten and to learn things I never knew.

"I thought I wasn't going to like it, but to my surprise, I really do like City. College is turning out to be a good experience for me. I think now of my future and I know it's going to be a better one. And I owe it all to my babes Martha."

Such is the story of Luis (we his friends call him Louie) Garcia. It is with the deepest honor that I have had association with him and that I am able to include his life story here. May the best of luck and blessings be with him in his future life.

Louie was the first homeboy who ever took me up on my offer of a paid job writing his life story. Though the corporation, *La Nueva Frontera Neutral*, was pretty dormant just after the departure of Sparks, eventually I saved enough money to offer incentive to the homies to tell about where they had come from and how they started their college careers.

Admittedly this was not the idea of the writing project I mentioned in the last chapter, with personal guidance for the writers, but it was a modification which would inspire self-starting among those who could and would take that initiative. Louie can be very proud of himself for taking that first big step.

6 HOMIES FROM LA, RIVERSIDE, AND SAN YSIDRO

Besides Louie Garcia who is from LA, San Diego City College has become the site for the education of homeboys and homegirls from relatively far-flung locations such as Riverside and the San Ysidro area. Anyone from Riverside, which is more than one hundred miles away, must, of course, move to San Diego, but the students from San Ysidro, about fifteen miles from downtown San Diego, commute regularly to classes. Though Southwestern College is closer to San Ysidro, some students find it more convenient to use the straight-shot transportation afforded by the San Diego Trolley.

During the spring semester of 1983, I met Carl Quesada who had come to San Diego from the Casa Blanca barrio in Riverside. He was a student in one of my mathematics classes. After a few months we became friends since he had decided that he thought I was a pretty good teacher.

When I told him my idea for this book, he approved of it, but did not want to do any writing. He said he would be satisfied with whatever I would write based on an interview with him.

"I tried to rob a gas station," he said, "got busted, was paroled to San Diego. I heard about the EOPS program at the various colleges and said, 'Hey, I'll go for the money.' Then I found out I liked it—that it wasn't that hard.

"And the girls kept me smiling," he concluded with a jovial grin.

In the fall of 1983 we had so many homeboys and homegirls at City College that I could not possibly tell the stories of them all. Of course there were several from the neighborhoods near to the college, homies from Sherman, Logan and Shelltown, but in connection with the topic of this chapter, students from relatively distant places, I must mention three guys who came all the way from the San Ysidro barrio, sometimes indicated simply by "Sidro." Their involvement in college was a direct consequence of the San Diego Street Youth Program, the origin of which I referred to in Chapter 4.

Gato, Ben, and Freddie were in one of my math classes. When I got to know them, I learned that they had come to college under the guidance of Mr. Eddie Perez at the South Bay office of the Youth Program. They claimed to find it much more convenient to take the fifteen mile trip by trolley than to take the bus and transfer to another bus to get to Southwestern College.

Photo 11 - Carl Quesada from Riverside, Casa Blanca

I understand, however, that there are several other homeboys going to Southwestern with the encouragement of the Street Youth Program. Good fruit from a good source.

About the same time I met a young lady named Nonie. She was studying computer programming and business administration. She contributed the following description of the earlier days of her life. Nonie said that her purpose was to encourage others of her *raza* to improve their lives with hard work, piety, and education. Here is Nonie's tale.

"My life being a *chola* all started when I was in elementary school, sixth grade. I started to understand what *varrio* claiming was all about.

"I come from South San Diego, a *varrio* named Del Sol. This *varrio* started growing fourteen years ago. It's not very old. As I was growing older, I would watch two of my older brothers always getting into trouble, hanging out with their friends, writing their names and *varrios* with spray paint all over the walls, coming home late and all loaded off of drugs and always getting into trouble with the police. I thought that was the only way of life— to be tough.

"I wanted to dress like them. They would show me how to talk and dress. By the time I was in the seventh grade, I was already painting my eyes. That they didn't like, but they already had me dressing like a *chola* (homegirl). I was always talking like one, saying, '*Q-Vo*' or '*Que onda*, homes?' Or if it was another girl from a different *varrio*, I would tell her, '*Puro Del Sol rifa.*'

"I would find myself getting into a lot of trouble with girls from other *varrios*. I started hanging around with the ninth graders. To me, then, that was big. They seemed to be more into it than the seventh or eighth graders. My homegirls used to always tell me, 'Come on, Nonie, let's go hit up this *ruca* from Otay and mess her up.' I used to say, 'Let's go.' I used to always start it by saying, '*Que varrio?*' She would either be scared or would come on all brave by naming her *varrio*. If she did answer, it would start off with a one-on-one fight and end up with all my homegirls jumping her.

"I had a real close friend named Flaca (Skinny Girl). She was a cool homie. She and I used to always party together. Even though she was much older, we understood each other real well. I always looked up to her. Whenever a big *ruca* would try to pick on me, she was always there to back me up. That's only if they would be a lot bigger than I was.

"The way that the other homegirls and I used to dress, our clothes would always be neat and clean and sharply creased to the max. We wore Levis slit on the sides and stiffened with starch. You would never catch us wearing a dress or bright colors; we would always be in our Levis or khakis. Dark colored clothes are what we always wore. Black, long trench coats with our brims— that used to look *firme*.

"My homegirls used to call me Bambi, but I didn't really stick to that *placaso*. I just used my nickname which I grew up with, '*La Loca* Nonie *de Varrio* Del Sol Sur San Diego.' A lot of my homegirls used to always cap on me because I didn't own even one pair of pants that wasn't creased, packed, and stiffened with starch. They used to call me Forever Creases.

"We always wore black shoes or black sandals. If we wore any other color, we would stand out in the crowd so everyone just stuck to black. If anybody ever stepped

Photo 12 - Nonie from South San Diego, Del Sol

on our shoes, I remember all the homegirls saying, 'Trucha. Watch out where you're stepping,' even to our own homegirls."

Nonie goes on to tell about her involvement in clubs called The Memories and The Latin Angels "getting together, having picnics, ending with fights or riots."

Eventually she went to meetings to help the different barrios to unite. Other meetings influenced her and others to turn to religious values.

The death of her boyfriend when she was sixteen was the main element which, as she puts it, "got it into our heads that this wasn't for us and into our minds to have a career and goals for the future."

"After my boyfriend was killed," she says, "I just couldn't face it all anymore. It frightened me inside to hang out with the homeboys and think that the same thing might happen to any one of them."

So she is now finishing up at City College and planning to continue her education at San Diego State University.

As final representatives of the hearty souls who travel relatively long distances to attend City College, I would like to mention Manny Dominguez and Rigo Reyes who are also from the South Bay area. I met Manny outside one of his classes at City College and learned that he is one of the partners who put out the magazine *Vivo*, a popular magazine similar to *Q-Vo* and *Lowrider*. I seem to recall that Manny said he's majoring in business.

My meeting with Manny was quite a coincidence because I already knew another of the *Vivo* partners, Rigo Reyes. In fact Rigo read the first eighty pages of this book and liked it so much that he contributed his own story. It is so impressive that I will use it as the end of this chapter about homies from barrios relatively distant from City College.

"My name is Rigoberto Reyes. My homies call me Rigo. Discrimination has followed me since I can remember. I don't intend to dramatize my experiences, but only wish to share my educational background.

"In junior high I was looked down upon by some teachers and administrators because of the way I dressed and talked; no encouragement was given to me to further my education past the high school level.

"To be honest, I never looked at college as an alternative. Nor did my homeboys for that matter. I always felt unwanted; administrators told me I was a trouble-maker, ditcher, fighter, *pachuco*, etc.

"My education at college started the same year I graduated from high school. It wasn't easy dealing with complicated college-level English that I had never been exposed to. Classes were hard. So I dropped out of Southwestern College in the middle of the semester. I felt pressured and uncomfortable. I was looked down upon again, this time by some administrators and some students, to my surprise, mostly by Chicano-Mexicano students. I felt the stares, talking behind my back— 'What is he doing here...Watch our cars start disappearing now...How can they let *cholos* in this college?' et cetera, et cetera. I guess it just got to me since I was about the only homie going to Southwestern College at the time.

"There was no one I could relate to. I wore khakis, a Pendleton, and a bandana, which are all part of my culture. I had refused and still refuse to assimilate to the white American culture. Perhaps that was the reason I was being rejected.

[Editor's Note: Rigo refers here to the very complex phenomenon of the relationships of the homeboys within the Chicano community. As Nonie noted above, in the junior high and high school grades, she would have been strange, out of place, if she had not dressed as a *chola*, but at the college level there is a different pattern and, of course, the pattern varies from school to school and college to college. If Nonie had attended school in some other part of the state of California or in a part of the US where there are fewer people of Mexican descent, she might have felt otherwise about her garb.

At the college level, the situation is quite different. Even though Rigo was going to Southwestern where the Chicano population is far higher than at any other San Diego area institution of higher education (thirty percent according to 1983 statistics), yet the attitude of Chicanos attending college is not always sympathetic to the *cholo* lifestyle. Perhaps they feel *cholo* garb should be outgrown before college matriculation. Or perhaps they are from that portion of the Chicano community which scorns *cholismo* and believes it should be ignored or obliterated.

The attitude among the students at City College seems to this observer to be more liberal and tolerant than what Rigo encountered at Southwestern. And maybe the attitude at Southwestern has liberalized as more homeboys attend there.

Of course the question of dress is a matter of fashion and we all know how the predominant society pressures people to dress for their part in life. What one would wear digging ditches would not be appropriate if one were working in a carpeted office. Even if co-workers were accepting toward such attire, the person wearing something unusual would feel uncomfortable. I can remember my own mother telling me, "Dress nicely and you will feel good about yourself." And, of course "nice" in this case means something appropriate for the occasion.

School administrators used to wrestle with the question of a dress code, thinking that it was their duty to help students prepare themselves for the public workplace. But nowadays the students set their own dress standards both personally and by reason of the interaction between themselves, i.e., by intergroup pressure. That is the pressure which Rigo was feeling. Life is a constant give and take between the peoples of the world and the only way to avoid it is to withdraw into isolation. Since no one wants to do that, we must come to the realization that every human relationship is a matter of minor politics and the most comfortable course is to learn to be diplomatic and tolerant.

Now back to Rigo's story.]

"I remember approaching the campus Chicano organization called MEChA, perhaps to find someone I could relate to. But in my opinion that particular group of students during that year was conservative, middle-class, and mostly concerned with the social sciences. It wasn't like I had remembered the MEChAs from the early 1970s at the peak of the Chicano movement. In my opinion it was an insult to see young Chicanos talking about cupcakes, cookies, the latest *chismes* (gossips), and parties under the name of *Movimiento Estudiantil Chicano de Aztlán*, i.e., MEChA. It was a turn-off, not at all what I had expected.

"These types of negative experiences made me leave college for two years. When I returned I was still confused, but determined to do something about those attitudes toward homeboys. I realized that I should get involved in human services, social services, and related fields.

"Since college I have worked in community-based agencies dealing with youth, primarily homeboys and homegirls. My involvement became constant and my concern for barrio violence grew. Because I grew up in the barrio, I am aware of and have been exposed to many different situations which happen every day in our communities. I have become a member of various grassroots organizations in San Diego. At the present time I am a member of Union Del Barrio, an organization committed to end barrio violence. I feel this organization is consistent with my first-hand awareness of the problems and conflicts found in dealing with Chicano youth.

"It was an unfortunate tragedy, the death of a very close friend, which prompted me and a group of friends to introduce a barrio-based publication, *Vivo* magazine, dealing with youth, barrio issues, and other community concerns. The idea had been discussed in the past, but the decision was made after the time in 1981 which left three young people dead in a period of two weeks. These youths did not deserve to die. The pain of their families cannot be forgotten. *We must search for alternatives to end this madness.* For these reasons we started *Vivo, La Vos Del Varrio*. Presently I am co-publisher and editor of this publication.

"I am not writing these lines to impress anyone, just with the hope that all Chicanos, homeboys or nonhomeboys, will start looking at each other as *carnales* and to encourage all the *Raza* to get involved in education, the political process, *cultura*, history, vocational trainings, etc.

"I am not glorifying the *cholo*-homeboy culture, nor do I condemn it. I am not ashamed to be from the barrio nor will I ever forget where I came from.

"I would like to leave you with this thought:

My *gente* says I'm a disgrace
because of the teardrop on my face.
The teardrop means *cinco balas*
that I did for a stupid *chavala*.
My *gente* says I'm a *cholo*,
yes, *pachuco*, homes, *vato loco*.

The gringo says I'm a wetback,
but I tell him, here, take that!
I am not a wetback!
I am just a proud Chicano
fighting for the big payback!

No te dejes, Raza!"

7 CONCLUSION

I feel, almost, that a conclusion is inappropriate for this book. This story is an on-going thing. As the sub-title indicates, the homies in this book and others like them, whose paths I have not crossed, are the Heralds of Progress, the start of the story rather than the story itself.

All that remains for me is to give a few final words of encouragement and admonition.

Education is like panning for gold. You find a few grains at a time, so little as to seem insignificant. Some days you find larger pieces which are tiny nuggets and they make you hopeful, but then there are days and weeks when only tiny specks are found. You are inclined to be discouraged, but you must keep your goal in mind and look to the future. If you persevere long enough and gather enough flecks of gold, someday you will be rich.

Discouragement comes to all of us. Realizing this, we should surround ourselves with people who support our goals. Most of us need friends who are positive, who will tell us, "Yes, I know, you have had a bad day and life is rough, but you are a tough person and I know you can do it if you keep on trying." We must not listen to the friends who make fun of our efforts or who do not believe in our goals. We must ignore those who want us to drink beer or smoke weed when we know we should be studying or pursuing whatever other good goal we may have.

Discipline is not a nasty word. Self-discipline is the key. No one can accomplish anything without it. It takes guts. But I never knew a homeboy who was not gutsy. Homeboys are willing to die for their barrios, but a dead homie never did anyone any good. Better to study for your barrio.

After a few hours of studying, you might find it so hard that you will say, "Hey, my barrio ain't worth all this trouble; it ain't even worth dying for."

But I say, "Yes it is, but most people are too selfish to do anything for their neighborhood. Most people study and live and, yes, die for themselves. They study so they can get a good job. They work for the bucks. They spend the money on themselves. They forget the parents and friends and teachers who helped them through childhood and encouraged them throughout adolescence.

"But the honor of a homeboy is more intense, better defined. He knows where his allegiance is due. With good education he can represent his people, a hard-working and noble-minded people with familial and community values. With job and money, he will have an honored position and that will demand respect, not only for himself, but for his *Raza*."

So I end this book, not so much with a conclusion as with a dedication. Here's to all the Heralds of Progress and also, not only to them, but to all those who will come after them. Theirs will be the next story written. Perhaps they will even write it themselves.

2014 AFTERWORD

Just after the first edition of this book hit the streets in 1984, I was assigned to teach math at San Diego State University. Though I observed only a handful of *cholos* at SDSU during those four years, the campus newspaper, *The Daily Aztec*, ran a front page photo and article about *Homeboys in College* in late '84 or early '85.

Thus when I met Jose Brosz at SDSU, he was very accepting of me and interested in my work with homies in LA and San Diego. He said he was from the South Bay area, the same barrio as both Rigo and Nonie—Del Sol.

He was working in construction when he got married. His wife's sister was a teacher. One day his wife said, "I'm going to quit my job and go back to school at City College."

Jose said, "Not without me. You'll run off with some smart f—er and I'll never see you again."

So in about 1978 they both went to San Diego City College and then on to San Diego State University where his wife went into elementary education and Jose focused on becoming a school administrator.

He earned a master's degree in educational administration. I have followed his stellar career as he has served as assistant principal and then principal at several different schools in the Sweetwater Union High School District.

Photo 13 - Mr. Jose Brosz, Otay Ranch High Principal
Photo from 2014 Otay Ranch High Newsletter

Jose Brosz is currently the principal at Otay Ranch High School which is located in Chula Vista. I was deeply gratified that, after thirty years, he still remembered me, my book *Homeboys in College*, and the picture of Gato, Ben and Freddie on the cover.

Here is an excerpt from his statement from the fall 2014 Principal's Message at ORHS.

"Our instructional focus is to ensure the successful implementation of rigor and relevance, critical analysis and thought, and all higher level evaluative skills, which are necessary in this technology driven era."

Jose says he has lived a blessed life as not only a proud Chicano *pachucho*/homeboy, but by my estimate, a humble and productive one as well.

Rigoberto Reyes (Chapter 6) has evolved from a youth who felt like an outcast to an adult who has promoted causes focused on the beauty and creativity of the Chicano culture. His story told us how the deaths of close friends and community members prompted him to leadership. Starting with promotion of San Diego's famed Chicano Park and *Q-Vo* magazine, then speaking his mind in numerous barrio/political organizations and the college academic world, he has accomplished marvels.

In my previous book *Hopie and the Los Homes Gang: A Gangland Primer*, I distinguish between homies, car club members, and members of Chicano social clubs. These are the three main, fairly-easily-distinguishable social groups within the American Chicano population. Americans of Mexican or Latin-American heritage who are not identifiable as being in one of these three groups have simply amalgamated themselves as new contributions to the vast American melting pot.

By becoming a prominent presence in every one of these Chicano and other San Diego organizations, Rigo has made his mark. His participation in Chicano social clubs and the educational community has resulted in a fabulous car club documentary called "Everything Comes from the Streets". Fittingly, though accidentally, it is hitting theaters in 2014 just as this second edition of *Homeboys in College* is released.

The film shows Rigo and many others in the San Diego community with their stunningly-restored cars. Shining with polished-wax finishes and rigged to the max with hydraulic shock absorbers, they are called "Low Riders" because the drivers, with the flip of a switch, can make the chassis of each car rise more than a yard high, then settle all the way to the ground. They can drive that way, making the car rise or fall (front, back, or both at once) or tip from side to side as they "cruise" through the streets.

Rigo is co-producer with Dr. Alberto Pulido of the school of Ethnic Studies at the University of San Diego. The award-winning film originated from a vast team at-or-associated-with KPBS-TV, San Diego's public broadcast outlet.

The film is already winning awards. Dr. Pulido says that he and Rigo are traveling nationwide to presentations which started in 2013 and continue through 2014 and beyond.

Jorge (Chapter 3) and his brother Alberto have settled in Michoacán, Mexico. His father, Augusto Torres, gave me his phone number.

Garrulous Jorge has adopted his father's profession. Thus he is making his living as a barber. His friendly and loquacious nature continues to please all.

As previously mentioned, Jorge forbade me to write Shady's story. Maybe Jorge will retire someday and write *The Tale of Jorge and Shady*.

For now I will say this much about Gaetano (Shady) Ulloa. He was and is my best friend of all, if it is possible to single out one from all of my favorite people. I used to talk to Shady about once a week and, even after I married and moved away from City College, we continued frequent contact for about four more years.

I visited his home several times and met his mother, father, sister and brother. Like Li'l Man had done, Shady came often to visit me and my growing family.

One day he told me about his girlfriend and his new baby. On several visits he borrowed money to buy diapers.

After I hadn't heard from him for a month or so, I called to see how he was doing. His sister answered. She said that Shady had moved to LA. He had a job up there.

Pretty soon the family phone was disconnected and they were gone without a trace.

In a similar way, I have lost track of lovely Nonie (Chapter 6) and most of the other guys. I wonder what has come of Chango, Topo, Diablo, and Smiley. Did they ever return to welding or some other training? And what about Gato, Ben, and Freddie? Though I never knew them well, their cover image for this book continues to inspire generation to generation.

Wherever you are Luis Garcia and Carl Quesada, my heart is with you.

Finally, to all of you stone-hard *cholos* out there, I love you and pray for you. I enlist the prayers and love of all of my readers for your advancement in goodness and wisdom, knowing as we all do that "the fear of the Lord is the beginning of wisdom".

If I may coin a phrase, "A college or trade school education is a step toward that wisdom."

Be one of the "Heralds of Progress!"

Made in the USA
San Bernardino, CA
15 May 2020